One Man's Meat

One Man's Meat

by

Sir Philip Joubert

FABER AND FABER
24 Russell Square
London

First published in mcmlxii
by Faber and Faber Limited
24 Russell Square London W.C.1
Printed in Great Britain by
Latimer Trend & Co Ltd Plymouth

CONTENTS

PREFACE

T he great gourmet Anthelme Brillat de Savarin in his essay —a long one—on the Physiology of Taste, makes it perfectly clear that there is an infinite variety of palates and tongues. He explains that the human tongue is not uniform and the number of 'taste buds' that dwell in it varies from individual to individual. This is a profound truth and explains the old saying: 'One man's meat is another man's poison'.

So, in the compilation of this book I must be forgiven if I have selected dishes and drinks which I have found personally agreeable or interesting. It would be only too easy to fault my selection —but it was my tongue, my palate, that made the choice. This must be my excuse if I find myself at odds with the Noble Order of Tastevins or the surviving members of that great company of gourmets who graced the tables of France in the years that are lost to us—for ever.

And if perhaps in this account I have come down rather heavily on the side of French cooking, remember that an ancient cookery book described the difference between English and French cooking by likening them to 'substance without sauce and sauce without substance'. I adore good sauces; like danger, they are the spice of life.

9

Preface

But this statement 'sauce without substance' is a very broad generalization. If a French and an English cook were given identical dishes to prepare I have little doubt that the Frenchman would produce something superior, in flavour and in presentation, to that offered by the Englishman. Recently I have read an article where the two forms of cooking were compared. The headline read, 'The British Gastronomes go to war against French culinary imperialism'. High time too, if we are to preserve our tourist trade! The article, however, did little but reaffirm the superiority of French cooking—in which, alas, I must from long experience believe. But here again is a generalization. I have dined in English private houses where the native cooking of our own dishes was superb. But go to a restaurant, a hotel or a café in the United Kingdom and what is offered is usually a blasphemy—not cooking.

So, I am mainly interested in what can be produced successfully in the kitchens of private houses.

Hence in the menus in the last part of this book I have tried to place myself in the position of the married couple, not too well off and very busy, but who still want to eat well from time to time. The type of menu assumes that for a large part of the year, plain food will be the order of the day, and so I offer only six special menus a month.

CHAPTER I

Cooking in General

C ooking originated when man first discovered how to control fire and put it to his own uses.

When this happened is not a matter of history—only of speculation. In the famous cave of the 'Red Rocks' on the French-Italian frontier a few miles from Mentone there are indications of human habitation over many thousands of years and the smoke of the cooking fire has stained the cliff walls for some hundreds of feet.

Primitive man no doubt had his feasts and in historical times there is a record of the many fantastic meals given by the emperors of the past. But it was not until about A.D. 50 that anybody tackled the problem of writing a cookery book. Up till then the master cooks had handed down their secrets by word of mouth to their successors.

In my researches amongst the valuable books in the London Library I first came across an indication of the existence of this cookery book, written by Marcus Gavius Apicius, who lived in the reign of the Roman emperor Tiberius. Like that of many other original thinkers. Apicius' work has been modified, developed and altered, not always for the best, by later commentators. The only manuscript of this book that has come through the years is the work of a plagiarist who lived in the late fourth or early fifth century A.D. He also called himself Apicius. The existing book in English, a translation from the false Apicius' original Latin text, by Barbara Flower and Elizabeth Rosenbaum, is probably a collection of recipes not all of which were the invention of Marcus Gavius Apicius. Nevertheless they give an excellent indication of the manner in which the wealthy Roman of the time of Tiberius and in later periods chose his meats. These were, in the main, material so pounded and mixed that it could be eaten with a spoon when reclining on one elbow on a couch, and with no taste left of the original basic matter. The explanation lies of course in the eating habits of the patrician Romans and the poor quality of the meat and game that came from the scanty pastures of their countryside.

There is no doubt that these principles of the Roman kitchen travelled across Gaul (France) and reached Britain after its conquest by Julius Caesar in 55 B.C. John Russell, in his *Boke of Nurture*, gives recipes which are very much akin to those of Apicius. The extensive use of spices such as ginger, cinnamon and cardamoms can only stem from a Roman root.

The quantities he quotes seem quite fantastic to our present day and age, but I hope by quoting a menu from a Lord Mayor's banquet of 1874 to show that, as compared with our grandfathers, we are 'poor, puddling eaters'—and probably all the better for it.

In one meat menu John Russell starts with a course of brawn with mustard, potage (presumably stock, herbs, spice and wine), beef, mutton, stewed pheasant, swan, capon, pork, boiled venison and a dish of pork that had been boiled in a bladder with eggs, pepper, cloves, currants, dates and sugar, and served with a rich sauce.

The second course contains two potages, a meat blancmange (what was this?), roast venison, peacock, partridge, woodcock, plover, egret and sucking rabbits. In the third course he writes of cream of almonds, curlew, snipe, quail and sparrows; perch in jelly, crayfish and baked quinces.

Finally a dessert of white apples, caraways, wafers and hippocras, a highly spiced red wine.

12

Cooking in General

He follows with a fish menu which is equally elaborate. It contains eighteen different types of fish interspersed with dates, jelly, almond cream, hot apples, ginger wafers and again hippocras to finish with.

It seems impossible that any one individual can have worked his way through such formidable menus, even taking small quantities. Perhaps the explanation lies in the long refectory tables at which the lords and ladies sat, each with the squire behind them. These many dishes would be set out in a row along the table, and only from what was immediately in front would the squire carve and serve his lord and lady on their trenchers of thick bread.

The chefs who cooked these vast meals were well paid. In Norman times the head chef could command a salary the equivalent of £3,000 a year of our present money. A large part of this was undoubtedly a bribe to prevent him from poisoning his lord!

It is most interesting to discover how many of the authors of these old cookery books look back at Greek mythology as a source of inspiration. Sometimes they even cull from old Indian legends. They were deeply read but, basically, the effect of food on the sexual organs was their main interest.

Endlessly they quote Latin and French tags such as 'A cook should be boastful. If he is quiet and modest he will be held to be a pitiful cook.'

Doran, in his book *Table Traits*, credits a number of royal ladies and noblemen with having actually created certain dishes which—even to this day—bear their names. The real inventors were probably undistinguished and unknown chefs living in the shadows of the kitchen.

English cooking did improve somewhat after the French Revolution at the end of the eighteenth century. Certainly some of the refugees of noble blood got down to the business of earning a living by cooking. One individual made a small fortune concocting vegetable salads that became very popular in London. But even until the 1840's a cook's reputation depended on his skill with pestle and mortar, and in the concoction of highly flavoured dishes that were 'fearfully and wonderfully made'. Gradually, however, the nineteenth century saw a general rational-

13

Cooking in General

ization of English cooking. The influence of French cooking, much improved since Roman days, began to be felt. Perhaps the Industrial Revolution which brought great wealth to a number of simple people, accustomed to plain roast and boiled, may have had some effect. But on occasion the quantities eaten were fantastic. This is the menu of the Lord Mayor's banquet of 1874.

SOUPS

Turtle. Clear Turtle.

FISH

Poudins de Merlans à la Francaise
Rougets aux fines herbes
Turbot. Cod. Smelts.

ENTREES

Crèpinettes d'huitres à la Creme
Gratin de Pluviers à la Chasseur
Turban de ris de veau aux truffes

REMOVES

Lark Puddings.
Turkeys and Celery Sauce. Roast Chickens.
Hams.
Saddle Mutton.
Procession of Baron of Beef, Plum Pudding, Boar's Head and peacock.

ROAST

Partridges. Widgeon. Pheasants.

ENTREMETS

Serrines de Foie gras
Clear Jellies Bararois à la Moderne
Mince Pies
Patisserie à la Bonne Femme.

REMOVES

Plombierès à la Regence
Souffles glacés
Caviare.

14

Cooking in General

I give the spelling as it appears on the menu. There are some obvious errors.

The reference to lark pudding is interesting. Russell and other early writers constantly quote 'roast lark', 'lark poudding' and lark in other forms. There must have been many more larks then in England than are seen and heard today.

Now to consider the general philosophy of modern cooking and my own particular viewpoint in this matter.

There have been men like Brillat-Savarin who have enjoyed the delights of their national dinner table throughout the years. From their experiences they have written of the food which the magnificent cooks of their native land have provided for them. But, in a sense, they have been isolationists. Their outlook has been limited, and unlike the great travellers of the past they have not that broad knowledge of how the world eats which would make of them a gastronomical encyclopaedia. Alas! Such travellers have, to my knowledge, not handed down to us the story of how they ate at ports of call during their expeditions. Eric the Red leaves no trace of how he fared on the coasts of Greenland. Nor does Christopher Columbus, nor indeed Doctor Livingstone, express any opinion on the manner of cooking and the material of the meals that must have been needed to keep them alive. Marco Polo could have told us so much about Chinese cooking.

In consequence, each nation has tended to prepare its food in its own particular way, and the cookery books follow the same pattern. There is one qualification, however, that needs to be applied to this broad general statement. Running like a thread through the weave of European cookery is the influence of the Chinese chef. Serious students of the art of gastronomy are prepared to admit that in the preparation, the cooking and the presenting of food the Chinese are supreme. There are strange and perhaps outrageous 'delicacies' in their menus—shark-fin soup, hundred-year-old eggs, swallows' nest *consommé*, and other highly flavoured dishes. But I well remember a meal in a Chinese house in Singapore which, so far as the entertainment was concerned, ranks very high in my estimation. My charming hostess, replenishing each guest's plate the moment his attention was turned elsewhere, and using a pair of porphyry chop-sticks for the purpose, made the threat to the digestion *une douce violence*. But I never understood how some of the American guests at this banquet could shovel great chunks of clam meat into their mouths and swallow the lot with a gulp of 'Scotch on the rocks'.

Of course Chinese influence spread more rapidly to the rest of the Far East than to Europe, Scandinavia and so on. Nevertheless, in very many cities in the West the Chinese restaurant, presenting Chinese food, is one of the features of social life today. In fact it is taking the place of 'the little restaurant in Soho where, my dear fellow, you get the best food in London'. The vogue in economical dining out is changing, and French, Italian and Greek *restaurateurs* are now under heavy competition from these intruders from Cathay.

Personally I don't like Chinese food. The Singapore dinner was an exception. After such a meal I feel like Montgolfier's balloon, full of air. An hour later I am hungry again!

Enough about Chinese food for the moment. What about the rest of the world?

I suppose the British service officer and man must have had more experience of strange meals than any other member of society. To begin with he is on the move roughly every three years, and in the days of our Far-flung Empire he could be expected to cover Europe, Asia, Africa and the Americas. To catalogue all the military posts that existed before the Hitler War would be a considerable labour, but a few examples will suffice. Attaché posts in the capitals of Europe and more lately the military missions—Gibraltar, Malta and Egypt in the Mediterranean—our colonies and our dominions, reaching from Africa, through India, Burma, Malaya to Hong Kong, to Australia and New Zealand, and westward to Canada, the U.S.A. and the West Indies. In each case a difference of climate, clothes and diet, and —most notably—of beverages. Business men from Britain are seldom long enough in any one place to begin to understand the local food and drink. Those that work in a particular country are limited in their experience. But the service man stays long enough in each place to savour it to the full, and then moves on, very

16

literally, to pastures new. He may have to swallow a sheep's eye at a tribal gala on the Indian frontier, but on the other hand enjoy a first-class meal in Hong Kong. He may have to drink sherbet in Kabul, but there is or was excellent claret in Bangkok. Pleasant or not, these are always worth-while experiences. It is from such experiences that I have built up my own philosophy of eating and drinking.

CHAPTER II

The Beginning of Experience

The first place where I ate or drank anything was in India —in the town of Calcutta, since I was born there. The reply to an American woman who asked why I was born there was simply that my mother happened to be there at the time. Now this mother of mine was an exceptional housekeeper, and although it is improbable that at any time in her life she ever did as much cooking as is involved in the boiling of an egg, she kept the best table in the upper hierarchy of India's social life.

She achieved this end by taking an infinity of pains over her daily menus. Her Mohammedan cook, while worshipping the ground upon which she stood, earned every pice that he was paid. The standard of the dinners never varied. The Commander-in-Chief or the Lieutenant-Governor fed no better or worse than the merchant marine apprentices from the shipping in the harbour who were my mother's periodical guests. One of these boys, who had never seen a finger bowl or ice cream before, achieved fame in the family annals by pouring the ice into the finger bowl, stirring it round with a spoon, and then drinking it off. He pronounced it champion.

One of the *spécialités de la maison* was liqueur chocolates. They were so good that at a tennis party where they were served at the tea-buffet on the lawn a young clergyman really went to town on them. Suddenly he was called away to take part in a game. Stuffing a handful of the chocolates into a trouser pocket, he dashed off. The game was long, the day hot. The chocolates melted and the curate was disgraced.

Here is one way in which these chocolates can be made by those who care to take the trouble to do so. First the liqueurs: use brandy, kümmel, chartreuse both green and yellow, indeed almost any liqueur provided it is not too sweet. Make your chocolate paste by melting unsweetened bar chocolate and mixing it in the proportion of half a pound of chocolate with a quarter of a small tin of evaporated milk. Spread the mixture fairly thinly on a flat surface and leave it to stiffen. Mix the liqueur into a thick paste with caster sugar. Mould the chocolate into a cup shape, fill with the liqueur mixture, and cover with a flap of chocolate to seal it. After a while the liqueur will separate from the sugar which acts as a lining to the chocolate. Chill in a refrigerator so that the chocolates harden nicely.

Of course curries figured very largely in the household menus. There is an idea very prevalent in England that all curries are so peppery that they can only be eaten by hardened orientals; further, that meat curry is the only one to make over here (to use up uneatable scraps) and that rice is difficult to cook.

Nothing is farther from the truth. Curries should first of all only be just peppery enough to create appetite, and no more.

But it is most important to give the curry powder a thorough cooking. If there is plenty of time, and in the preparation of curry the cook should always allow at least two hours, the meat, preferably fresh steak, the chicken, the vegetables, the eggs and the fish should first be lightly fried or boiled. Place the basic ingredient (as above) aside, and in the case of meat curry, in a big frying-pan prepare the onions that give the flavour. As soon as the onions are well cooked add the meat together with sliced apple, raisins, a touch of tomato *purée* and a tablespoonful of chutney. Finally put in the curry powder with plenty of stock and leave to simmer, covered up, for at least an hour, preferably more.

19

With the chicken proceed as above. Fish and egg do not need the onion.

Now the rice. It *must* be good Patna type. This is essential and the small extra cost is well worth while. Boil in plenty of water with salt and a couple of bay leaves for exactly fifteen minutes. Wash and drain in a colander and, on a plate, put the colander into a slow oven for five minutes. The rice will then be in separate grains and in perfect condition for eating. It is just as simple as that!

But curry by itself is not the complete curry meal. In Malaya and in the former Dutch East Indies as many as a hundred different herbs and spices are served with curry. These vary from dried and rather smelly fish, chillies, gherkins and grated coconut to the agreeable thin biscuit known as the puppadam. All those mentioned above can be bought in England. Unless, however, you are in the position of a Siamese diplomat I knew who received his supply of these special herbs by air in the diplomatic bag, you are unlikely to obtain the other kinds.

Then there is the dish that should follow the curry to take away all trace of 'bite' remaining on the tongue. In south-east Asia a concoction known as 'gula malacca' is served. So far as can be discovered by the passing traveller this seems to be semolina with a treacle or melted brown sugar sauce. It is soothing and not too cloying. Banana fritters can serve the same purpose.

I have written of fairly simple curries within the powers of the unambitious cook. But there are others. Some years ago I had a friend, the aforementioned Siamese diplomat, who imported his herbs by air. He and his lovely wife agreed to prepare for me something very special in the curry line. Actually the charming Nu did all the work while Chin looked on and approved. The dish was to be served at my house and in due time a car arrived and disgorged Chin, Nu and the following articles. Item one: a large copper dish in which were bits of the finest chicken. Item 2: a large bowl containing mussels in a curry sauce. Item 3: a mountain of steaming rice on a huge platter that was edged with slivers of carrot cut into attractive patterns and with spring onions trimmed to look like tiny palmtrees.

The Beginning of Experience

This combination of mussels, curry, chicken, rice and raw vegetables to cool the tongue was something none of the gastronomes who ate it will ever forget. Nu was a superb cook. Trained in the art as one of the Siamese Royal Family in the famous school of deportment at Bangkok, one of her tasks was to peel and stone a bunch of grapes without removing the fruit from the stem. 'Of course,' said Nu, 'you have to use a gold knife!'

The drink to take with curry is, of course, draught beer. It has exactly the right taste, simple and unexciting, to follow the complications of the dish. What is equally important is to eat your curry with agreeable companions. I remember an occasion at the Naval Base in Singapore in 1938 when, with a dish piled high from the rice and curry table, and with a tankard of cool beer in my hand, I was placed between two of the prettiest women in the island. And not only pretty but intelligent! To my deep regret, after the meal I had to attend a rather dreary conference, leaving them to the further pleasure of the afternoon siesta!

But I am running ahead of my story. After leaving India at the age of nine I was sent to a very rough private school in the south of England. Here the food was simply abominable. On one occasion the meat was brought into the dining-hall and immediately ordered out by the master on duty. It was quite rotten! So we lunched on blue boiled potatoes and sloppy greens. The headmistress had boasted to my mother that feeding 120 boys was very cheap. It cost sixpence a day per head. Well we knew it!

Even at a very well-known public school which later I attended, my parents had to give me 15s. a week so that I could buy extra food and milk. This subvention, though perhaps not on the same lavish scale, was common form throughout the school. Holidays were a joy! At least one could eat one's fill of good food. Home-baked bread (Mary, the Irish cook, was an expert) is something almost unknown to this modern world. The dull products of the mass-producing factories of today are just tolerable and hardly nourishing. But a crusty loaf fresh from the oven was something to look forward to with pleasure.

In the south of France where I spent my Christmas holidays with a friendly aunt the food was out of this world. Philippe, the Alsatian cook, was a master of his art. His oven was an enormous cast-iron affair, burning coke and wood. In the morning a dozen little copper pots, filled with stock and various herbs, would be simmering on its black and gleaming surface. Here was the basis of good French cooking, the sauces that were to add flavour to meat, game, and fish, later to be cooked in the ovens.

CHAPTER III

Further Experiences

It was in my aunt's house on a certain Thanksgiving Day in the early 1900s that I had my first introduction to the American attitude to food. My aunt had invited a number of her American friends to lunch and as it was a United States festival the cook, Philippe, had really 'pushed the boat out'. He had prepared a magnificent crayfish which he served cold. The meat was carefully sliced and replaced in the shell. Around the dish was an elaborate decoration of green and red vegetables and the whole made a pretty picture. Small new potatoes, hot, and a cold mayonnaise were served with the fish.

One after another the Americans either refused altogether or just picked at the dish. When pressed, one of them helped herself to potatoes, cucumber and lettuce! Complete disaster, and why? It must have been the tradition that all shell-fish outside the U.S.A. were and are contaminated with typhoid germs. Less than three years ago a Yankee friend of mine rang me up to inquire whether the water served at the Berkeley Hotel was safe to drink. Since her arrival in England she had been quenching her thirst with Perrier or Evian water!

I shall have more to say on this subject later on.

After leaving Harrow in 1904 I went for a short while to a

crammer's and, having passed my examinations, joined as a gentleman cadet (almost an officer and not quite a gentleman as the saying went) the Royal Military Academy, Woolwich. Here it must be said that the food was good, ample in quantity and well presented. Grace said by the Senior Under Officer on duty 'For what we are about to receive—Thank God—sit down!' was no empty promise. And then two years later to Aldershot as a second lieutenant in the Royal Field Artillery. The only outstanding event during my stay in the Wellington Barracks there was the alarm caused by the officer in charge of messing. Taking his opportunity when the majority of the officers were on manœuvres, he regaled himself, and one or two others who were also left to 'hold the fort', on oysters and champagne. The bill was presented when we returned, and 'we were not amused'.

And then to Woolwich—the Headquarters of the Royal Regiment and one of the best messes in the world at this time. Every subaltern joining the Regiment paid £3 to the Woolwich Mess funds and thus became entitled to mess membership for life. I was reminded of this agreeable fact a few years ago when I had cause to lunch there. The standard was as high as ever. It was during my three years at Woolwich, 1909 to 1912, that I spent a very happy time at table. Here for a daily charge of 4s. 6d. we were offered at breakfast porridge or cereal, two kinds of fish, kedgeree, cold ham, bacon, eggs in any required form, kidneys, sausages, tea or coffee. Lunch was a three-course meal, excellently cooked, while at dinner the really serious eating of the day was undertaken. There were never less than four courses served on the mahogany tables that were decorated in the centre with magnificent silver ornaments and lined along their borders with baize underfelt and strips of Irish linen. After the savoury was cleared away the 'white waiters', dressed in cream surcoats embroidered with red, red waistcoats and cream knee breeches took post at the top and bottom of each table. The butler gave a signal and the strips of baize and linen were seized and twisted till they represented a parti-coloured sausage. At another signal the waiters in the prescribed positions would give a straight pull, and the 'sausages' would end up on the floor without disturbing a single ornament. As the tables were about thirty feet long, this was quite a feat.

On the edges of these tables there was a four-inch extension of some antiquity. The story goes that the Prince Regent, who dined frequently in the mess, became so drunk on one occasion that he fell under his table. There he was joined by another officer who, most unfortunately, rowelled the Royal Face with his spurs. Next day the Mess President received a command to the effect that as his tables were not wide enough for a gentleman to get drunk under in comfort their width should be increased.

As regards the mess cellar I got into trouble once in the matter of wine. I had discovered an unnamed claret costing 1s. 3d. a bottle and proceeded to drink it regularly at dinner. About a month later the butler came to me and said, 'Sorry, sir! You can't have any more of that wine. That's for the senior officers, that is!'

The Woolwich mess was renowned for its drinks. Careful buying of young wines throughout the years had kept the prices low, and after prolonged maturing in the deep cool cellars, a produce satisfactory in every respect was available for drinking. So deeply ingrained in the cellar staff was this feeling of perfectionism that even when the Hitler War threatened the wines were not moved to a safer place. They would have been disturbed and so lost some of their quality. Providence looked after the cellar. Only one bomb hit it and that did not explode, but several dozen of old brandy were lost. A club I know panicked in 1939 and sold off many dozens of Taylor's 1924 port at 2s. a bottle! The building was never touched and six years later the same port was selling at over 40s. a bottle.

I regret to say that during my time at Woolwich I never inquired into the manner of preparing all the excellent food I ate. If I had, I should probably have been severely snubbed, first by the head cook and then by the mess secretary for interfering with the staff. Later, when, in December 1912, I joined the Royal Flying Corps, the mess food was so ordinary as to provoke no interest. Then came the Kaiser's War, and one's chief interest was to get enough food of whatever sort to avoid going hungry. It is often forgotten that one result of Germany's successful sub-

marine campaign was to bring south-east England to the verge
of starvation. A posting from France to the home establishment
in that area meant very short commons indeed.

One thing I learnt about cooking when in France in the autumn
of 1914 was how to make a chicken casserole. This dish was
prepared by a brother officer—an Australian—in the open and
cooked on a wood fire. The basis was a young cockerel that he
had, with some difficulty, persuaded a local farmer to sell him!
The bird, duly plucked and drawn, was first lightly cooked in a
little water, in which small onions, herbs and salt had been placed.
It was then cut up into small pieces, a little red wine added to the
stock, and then the casserole, firmly covered with its lid, was
buried in the hot ashes. After about three-quarters of an hour our
dinner was served and it was excellent. Up till then one of the
airmen had been cooking for us, but when we found his boots
and socks in the same box as our bread and bacon, a change had
to be made and the Australian took over the job.

I have often wondered why in England it is so difficult to buy
young vegetables, in particular tiny marrows. They are available
in big towns but rarely in the country. Abroad, and especially in
Egypt where I was serving in 1916, they can be bought when they
are only a few inches long. Lightly boiled, split and stuffed with
a savoury mince, and then grilled or fried, they make the most
excellent eating. The cry of the hawker calling '*Courgie blanc,
courgie noir*' would bring our mess sergeant in a run to the door.
Even bully beef tasted better when treated in this way, as stuffing
for a *courgette*.

Rizottos were also a great stand-by, when we were in Italy
during 1918. The standard ration of bully beef and bread tasting
faintly of paraffin (the rations and the oil travelled together in the
same lorry) was discouraging to the appetite. So MacCarthy, our
cook, set himself the task of learning Italian cooking. Rice was
plentiful and so three or four times a week we ate rizotto.

Now there were many variations that can be played on this
well-known theme. MacCarthy did not aspire to greatness in the
matter and his rizotto was the usual fairly dry rice, steeped in

Further Experiences

tomato juice and trimmed with grated parmesan cheese. But this form can pall after a while. There is great scope for imagination in the preparation of rizottos so I give but one example:

In a frying-pan prepare a sauce consisting of melted butter, a little milk or stock, a tablespoonful of tomato *purée*, chopped fresh chives and parsley. Stew this for twenty minutes, taking care to keep it moist; meanwhile, boil your rice in a separate pan. Add chopped meat to the frying-pan five minutes before your rice goes into the oven for drying.

Quantities of course vary according to the number of diners, but for two use a breakfastcupful of rice, three ounces of meat, and a small quantity of chives and parsley.

While in Italy I met a Major Wilkinson, a member of the Intelligence Staff at G.H.Q. We became good friends and when, after the war, I was posted to Oxford we met frequently in his rooms at Worcester College. With him I learned a good deal about the art of drinking port. He had access to a small supply of 1887 Coburn which, in 1919, was still in first-class condition. At thirty-two years of age it was approaching its decline, but since it had never been moved, it had survived longer than the normal span. I regard twenty-five years as this span and in the twenty-fifth year a good vintage port is at its prime. I drank some Coburn 1912 in 1935 and it was perfection. In that same year I was offered some 1856—the Comet port. Far too old, it was like a highly brandified sherry. But it must have been magnificent in the early 1890s.

France was, and in some places still is, the home of good cooking. In the years after the war Philippe the Alsatian ministered to my wants to my great satisfaction. But food in private houses is one thing. In restaurants it is quite another matter. It was in 1935 that for the first time I slept in a Frenchman's house—at his invitation.

It is an interesting fact that a foreigner may have many friends among French people, but he will not be asked to stay with them. As much entertainment in hotels, restaurants and night clubs as you please, but not in the sanctity of the home! And so most foreigners can only sample French hotel or restaurant cooking. Already past middle age, and with a long experience of France and Frenchmen, I breached this front in the following way. I was invited to be the guest of the French 'Fighter Command' of which the H.Q. was in Tours, the heart of France socially and gastronomically. After one day of my visit the Air Officer Commanding had had enough of me and farmed me out among his friends. They could not refuse him, so for the rest of my stay I was fed and bedded in private houses. This was a most fortunate affair as I made some friendships which have endured up to this day. In the houses of these friends I have eaten dishes and drunk wines that are not normally available to the stranger. The local wines don't travel, and in the days when the French Government was not so concerned about drunkenness it was possible to own a private still. In this machine that fiery liquor called 'marc' was distilled. A juice made from fermented fresh fruits, strawberries, raspberries, peaches, all pushed into a barrel, was called most appropriately 'Tutti-frutti' and nearly blew the top off one's head.

In one house the cook was a communist, but superb at her job. One sweet she served I have never seen before. Pancakes were piled on a dish to a height of at least fourteen inches. Each pancake was easily separable from the others and was stuffed with a delicious cream and jam filling. The skill required to build this erection so that it did not become a soggy mass, and remained piping hot as well, was that of a mistress of the art of cooking— no dish for the amateur. Other dishes that came from her hand are quoted later in the more technical part of this story.

As I moved from Tours to Rheims there was, of course, champagne to drink. Two brands I well remember. One came from a small estate, that of Piper, the product of which is not generally available. It was a 1915 which had never moved from my host's cellar and was most enjoyable. The other was a local red called Bouzy which will not travel. This brew is relatively cheap and most strongly recommended for drinking at 11 a.m.

I lunched with the owner of the '1915' and he gave me an ambrosial dish. It was called *Lièvre Cardinale* and I have never come across it again—to my great sorrow. As far as I could discover the

28

basis was the equivalent of our jugged hare. This meat was mixed with *pâté de foie gras*, truffles and pistachios. It was then rolled into a large sausage, larded and served cold. The hare meat had of course been marinated in burgundy, hence its red colour and its name!

Writing of French entertainment in hotels reminds me of two occasions which I remember well. It was also in 1935 that the French Air Force gave me lunch in Paris at the famous Café de la Paix, which—alas!—is no longer the resort of searchers after good living.

At this lunch we assembled at 12.30 p.m. for the usual aperitif —porto rouge, porto blanc: 'Un verre de Herez, mon général!' or a glass of delicious 'Blanc de blanc'. About one o'clock we sat down to an avalanche of *hors-d'œuvre*, which was followed by *sole au vin blanc*. The accompanying wine was a Meursault—only just chilled, not frozen as is so often the case in an English restaurant. Then there was duckling with a morello cherry sauce, green peas, new potatoes and a lettuce salad. With the duck was a delicious Burgundy, a Chambertin. Followed a *sorbet au maraschin* and then a respite of a few minutes during which conversation flowed in two languages, but on the one subject of food. Service matters were held firmly in abeyance. Soon a vast platter covered with a variety of cheeses was handed round and for those still able to drink there was that marvellous claret, Château Ausone. This comes from a small vineyard which produces a very limited number of barrels each year. But when the weather has been kind, the delicacy and bouquet of Ausone have every other claret beat!

Round about 3.45 coffee was served, with brandy, armagnac or sweet liqueurs. At 4.30 p.m. I staggered off to my hotel practically in a coma.

The other occasion was during my visit to Paris to attend the celebrations connected with the twenty-fifth anniversary of Louis Blériot's flight across the Channel on 25th July 1909. The French Air Ministry had prepared an enormous banquet in one of the big restaurants, and I, supposedly because I had flown Blériot aeroplanes, was seated next to Mme Blériot. I have no recollection whatsoever of what I ate or drank. For the whole meal I was in a state of acute embarrassment. At the same table was the Air Minister and with him two ex-Air Ministers. Mme Louis Blériot expressed her opinion of these gentlemen very loudly and in no measured terms. 'Why', she asked, 'were not large contracts given to the Blériot firm, the builders of the most famous aircraft in the world? It was a scandal that, due undoubtedly to *influences néfastes* other firms were being awarded lush assignments to build—what? *De la camelote!* Duds, my dear general, duds, and it is a public crime.' By contrast my A.D.C., seated between two pretty girls but not so far off as to be beyond my observation, had a wonderful evening. I may have been eating the stalled ox—but in an atmosphere of hatred. Much preferable would have been a dinner of herbs and the love the lad was enjoying!

Harking back to Touraine for a while, an interesting dish was served at a delightful little manor house some miles north of Tours. The main course, a delicious roast chicken, had a taste of wood smoke, which, curiously enough, was very agreeable and reminiscent of a barbecue. I had been into the kitchen earlier on and had noticed that the stove was a very modern Aga. How then the wood-smoke? My hostess explained, with a giggle, that it was very simple. As the bird was nearing perfection a smouldering twig of wood was passed round the inside of the oven and the smoke firmly closed in for some minutes.

CHAPTER IV

Between the Wars

Let us leave France for a while and move on to other countries. The period of recovery in Britain's economy after the Kaiser's War, despite the 1929–31 slump, was not unduly prolonged. By 1935, and at no great cost, it was possible to live comfortably and agreeably. Some figures are worth quoting. Good coke delivered at the house was 32s. a ton on the south coast of England. Coal was slightly more expensive but at least it was clean and free from stone and slate. Food was reasonable and there was a wide choice. Whisky and gin were round about 12s. 6d. a bottle according to quality. Beer was so cheap that I cannot remember its cost. Château-bottled clarets, at least ten years in the bottle, were 8s. A vintage port of 1924 was 12s. Champagnes, however, even by modern standards, were expensive. It was necessary to go to France before one could buy a good *Champagne Nature* for 15 francs—about 2s. 6d.

It must have been in 1936 that I had my first taste of prephylloxera claret, that is to say, vintages of the early seventies. In a friend's house, where I was spending the week-end with a few companions, six bottles of a superb vintage, corks drawn, were lined up by midday on the dining-room mantelshelf. By dinner

31

they would be at room temperature, and 'breathed', and thus in perfect condition for drinking. They were just that!

The business of buying, cellaring, maturing and then the ceremonial drinking of good wine is almost a forgotten art. Until the Kaiser's War people of substance bought wine by the cask on the recommendation of their wine merchant, bottled it and laid it down for an appropriate period in a cellar where the temperature varied only slightly from fifty degrees year in, year out. Some, who may have lacked cellar space for large quantities of port, bought it by the pipe and kept it in bond until it was fit for drinking. There were some superb years—1906, 1912, 1924, 1927— where clarets and ports alike were good or magnificent. But now the stock of fine wines has almost disappeared and nothing is coming forward to replace it. The decline of port began when the Portuguese Government of Dr. Salazar moved in on the British wine industry of Oporto. French wines suffered when the national desire for the quick turnover persuaded the vintners to initiate the practice of *égrappage*, the stripping of the grapes from the stalk before crushing. The result of this process was to reduce the tannin content of the young wine and so make it palatable in a very much shorter space of time than was possible if there was a lot of tannin to get rid of. But the quality of the wine suffered, and this I am prepared to swear in the face of all the arguments put forward by the 'trade'. The young stuff—three to five years old—that is now marketed has nothing like the body or the bouquet of the products of even the early 30s. There is still some good 1934 claret to be found and it is completely different from the 1947 which has been so much advertised because it was an enormous vintage.

The famous Doctor Pasteur devised a chemical way of maturing wine in as many months as the years necessary to do so by natural means. But nobody would drink his product. It was unpalatable.

In this connection I will have something to say later about American methods of preparing food for tins and packages, of plunging everything into the deep freeze, and of sterilizing and pasteurizing what they eat. It is much the same story—the quick turnover and the avoidance of care; the mechanization of the art of eating.

In the years before the Hitler War I had the opportunity to sample food and drink in Germany, Italy, Austria and Hungary. Frankly, I don't like German food. It is substantial and fortifying but lacking in charm. Even the Vierjarheszeiten Hotel at Munich had nothing to offer but copies of the menus of France as an alternative to the local dishes. Of the wines, there is of course hock, which can be wonderful, and the Palatinate brews that on the whole are too sweet for my taste. A Wachenheim Trocken Beeren Auslese is a formidable beverage. A wineglassful is enough to satisfy the normal palate. Of Austria my recollections are chiefly of Wiener Schnitzel and Sacher Torte of which one can have enough quite quickly. But evenings in a flower-draped *Keller* were enchanting. I am never tired of the Viennese waltzes and of the gay, friendly people who have survived invasion and two bitter wars without losing their *Stimmung*.

Hungary before the Russian occupation was a lovely place. Buda-Pest, rather shabby, with hotels where the plumbing was primitive and the woodwork lacked paint, was a thrilling place to visit. One bar offered eighty varieties of that famous wine, Tokay. I sampled half a dozen and concluded that it was merely rather an interesting white of which the best were good and the rest mediocre. Once, in other circumstances, I tasted the true Imperial Tokay that, like all of the very special whites, is made from late picked and sun-dried grapes. It is supposed to be a specific tonic for invalids recovering from pneumonia. As a beverage, it is heartening and has a faint aroma of brown bread!

Another Hungarian speciality is a white fish caught in Lake Balaton and called *forgash*. Among freshwater fish it can be classed as very good, something like turbot, but not so firm. When I tried it cooked in butter with fresh herbs and washed down with Tokay I enjoyed it very much.

There were of course the standard continental dishes and these were particularly well served at a restaurant on one of the hills that surround the town of Buda. At this place there was the usual gipsy band, flute and fiddle predominating. The flautist was, to my heated imagination, something out of the woods—Pan himself perhaps. A pair of sparkling black eyes shone from a yellow-white face and two pointed ears completed the illusion. He was playing with intent at a love-lorn couple seated near me, and, as I watched, the girl's eyes took on the look of a mesmerized animal—a moth perhaps, staring at a bright light. The rest of my party wanted to be off to the local night club, but I could not be moved. Here was witchcraft and I wanted to see what would happen. Alas! I was dragged away to a place with a revolving dance floor and a band playing the latest jazzy tunes!

Of Italian food I have little to say in praise. The basis— tomatoes, cheese and pasta! But on the coast there is quite a good dish called *Frutta Di Maré*. This consists of a stew of small fish, baby octopus and shell-fish, something akin to the bouillabaisse of Provence. The best wine to drink with it is a white Soave. Italian wines on the whole are poor stuff. Though the Romans were early in the wine-making and drinking business there has been little progress in viticulture and in the preparation of wine since their day.

CHAPTER V

The East

Aposting to India brought me new experiences at the table. My first introduction, or rather a reintroduction, to Indian food was most unhappy. The restaurant car on the express carrying me from Bombay to Delhi served food cooked in coconut oil. There is hardly anything more revolting in this world. The taste is acrid and the 'returns' catastrophic. I advise all travellers by train in the sub-continent to take their food with them.

Delhi, however, provided everything that was good. A special dairy farm run by a European sold good milk, meat was plentiful and of reasonable quality, and of course poultry, game and fish were abundant. Every English drink was available, port having to come all the way from Madras as the only place with a climate where the temperature does not vary greatly. It was here in an Indian household that I ate my first curry in which small quantities of gold and silver leaf were mixed. This practice is not 'swank', but is based on the theory that the metal makes the curry more digestible.

It was, however, in Afghanistan that my experience of food was considerably advanced. I had flown to Kabul with the Foreign Secretary, Sir Aubrey Metcalfe, who was negotiating a trade treaty with the government. To entertain their distinguished guest the Afghans had prepared a special luncheon at a delightful spot called Paghman in the foothills of the Hindu Kush. The meal was served in a large marquee and began with an excellent chicken soup in which were mixed a few almonds, pistachios and raisins. The soup bowl was an enormous gourd coated with thick pastry, and undoubtedly some of the 'meat' of the gourd had been added as thickening. Then followed three different kinds of pillau, meat, chicken and fish. Feeling full fed already I asked my neighbour, an English-speaking Afghan, if there were to be any more courses. 'Yes, indeed,' he replied, 'now comes the sheep cooked in a cave.' This was a whole lamb, roasted on hot stones in a hole in the ground! It was really excellent and I had to find space for a mouthful or two! Finally there was ice-cream and an abundance of fruit. Being a Moslem country, no alcohol was served—only sweet sherbet! This brew combined with the pillaus to produce a feeling of distention of truly remarkable proportions!

Trips to Gilgit in the Karakoram mountains and to Kashmir were notable for the local trout, caught and cooked within three hours. Such trout are entirely different from the aged specimens, coming perhaps from a Norwegian fiord or a Danish lake and shipped on ice to England that are for sale in Britain. They closely resemble the *Truite au bleu* that one can eat in a Swiss restaurant in the mountains—caught and cooked within the hour. The flesh is still firm and has kept all its flavour. One must never forget the little blob of fat that lies just behind the eye—it has its special charm.

When I was in India as a child I thought the fruit wonderful. Grapes from Kabul packed in wooden baskets—each grape separate in its bed of cotton wool; fresh litchis from the hills, juicy and translucent when freed from their brown and prickly shells; oranges; ex-patriate apples (with little flavour); pineapples from Burma; bananas (those from Bombay the best); and mangoes in their season, were all well regarded. A generation and more later when I went back these did not satisfy. There is no question at all, in my opinion, that fruit grown in Britain is the best in the world, and the rest, by comparison, are inferior. This is particularly the case in Malaya where the exotic-looking fruits are almost tasteless, probably due to the heat and excessive humidity. It appears that the durian is a local delicacy, but the attitude of a waiter at the well-known Raffles Hotel in Singapore when I asked him for a slice, confirmed the rumour I had heard: that the durian smells strongly of drains.

There are some good fish to be had in Bengal. The becti and the mango fish, the one somewhat like turbot and the other a largish smelt, are quite worth eating. Oysters and crayfish are to be found at Karachi and perhaps elsewhere, though I have never heard of another source. Most Indian fish, however, are best disguised in a curry.

Game birds are plentiful, the best being teal, snipe and ortolan. There are many other varieties, all more or less eatable. Among the domestic fowls the Indian chicken is in a class by itself. Small, stringy and in a perpetual state of semi-starvation it is hardly surprising that the eggs the hen lays are about as big as marbles, and that a whole cockerel would hardly satisfy one diner. It is amazing, though, what the Indian cook can do with this un-promising material. This leads me to a description of the Indian kitchen which indeed is the pattern for kitchens all over the East.

In a mud hut thatched with palm leaves a hearth, also made of dried mud, stretches across the full width of the building. In this hearth there may be as many as a dozen holes in which charcoal is burning. The draught is maintained by a small boy waving a palm-leaf fan and the smoke goes out through the holes in the walls. Spread along the edge of the hearth are the cook's pots and pans, mainly made in Birmingham, though there will be a bazaar-made brass lotah holding water. In a corner will be the earthen-ware water container and on a low shelf the materials for the meal. There will be quite a lot of flies about the place, and scouting outside the inevitable mangy pariah dog.

It is indeed quite amazing how, with such elementary equip-ment, a good Indian cook can produce an excellent meal of several courses for as many as a dozen people. My cook Shafr-U-Din was not only good at his job, but also very clean. There were few flies and less dirt in his kitchen and no pariah dog. Nobody in the house ever suffered from tummy trouble. For two winters in Delhi he made my dining-room a most popular rendezvous for both seniors and juniors. After one Christmas dinner a distinguished visiting scientist, having some difficulty with his speech, assured me that it was the most wonderful meal he had ever eaten.

I admit with shame that I never watched Shafr-U-Din to see how he managed his affairs. I could have breathed down his neck while he did his roasts and boiled, but orientals are a bit sensitive about their association with Europeans and it is very easy to offend them. So, apart from congratulations on a particularly successful meal, our relationship was one of courtesy and reserve.

My time in India came to an end when the Hitler War broke out. Posted back to England in October 1939, I still kept in touch with my Delhi friends. Life there seems to have gone on undisturbed for quite some time because, just before the daytime blitz started in August 1940, I received a letter of considerable interest. 'You will hardly believe it but the same routine of golf, tennis, bowls, cocktail parties, dinners and dances still goes on. In fact we are being very neutral out here!'

At home, however, the restrictions imposed under Government orders by Lord Woolton at the Ministry of Food were already being felt. Though the shortages of 1917 were far more painful, there were now many articles and—more particularly—quantities of certain foods that it was impossible or illegal to buy. The need for these restrictions was obvious. From September 1939 the impact of Germany's unlimited submarine campaign was far from negligible. As the submarine fleet grew in numbers so did its successes. America hardly suffered at all, being largely self-sufficient in foodstuffs. Britain bore the burden. France starved but from another cause—the occupation.

Personally I was little affected. First living at a club, the secretary of which seemed to manage very well, then at an operational headquarters where I drew rations for the family and three batmen, I did not feel the pinch. Only when Sir Stafford Cripps came to lunch had something to be done very quickly about the milk supply! Later, two years in India and Ceylon, living more than comfortably, did not prepare me for the austerity of England in the immediate post-war years. It was then that, in retirement, I really began to learn about the preparation of food sufficient to keep body and soul together on minimum supplies. Eggs, butter, meat and bacon were the real problems. The supply of eggs was solved by purchasing half a dozen pullets and during the first year I reckoned the eggs cost me about 14s. a dozen. On the chicken house alone I spent £15, and meal was also very dear. But the 'girls', as we called them, laid so well that we could even supply our friends. Potatoes were a magnificent stand-by and later I give a number of recipes for their preparation. Once we inherited a whole sheep, which we cared for on the lawn. Tony Lumbkin became a real friend and it was a terrible day when he had to be slaughtered. We all left the house and returned in the evening heavy-hearted. I swore I could never eat any of him, but the butcher telephoned some days later saying that Tony looked so different now I would feel better about him. But it was not until an avalanche of friends descended upon us that we nerved ourselves to send for the meat.

During the years that have followed I worked hard at the business of cooking and in the end became most interested. My wife and I were constantly experimenting, sometimes successfully. We were never content to take the recipes set out in our cookery books, but introduced modifications which appeared to be improvements.

One outstanding event in our cooking saga was a visit to America. Its details are set out in the chapter that follows, including our views on the eating and drinking habits in that great country.

CHAPTER VI

No Icebergs in My Glass

On an evening in late December 1956 our ship, after a very stormy Atlantic crossing, crept up the East river and so to New York. We had passed through quarantine, having discussed the breeding of bull-terriers and the wearing of regimental ties with a friendly official. It is usually helpful when travelling abroad to conduct such entirely irrelevant conversations with functionaries of almost every country since they tend to distract and divert inquiries from more pertinent matters such as vaccination and contraband certificates! Dusk was falling as Manhattan Island came in sight. Office and apartment windows were glowing and by some trick of the atmosphere they showed coloured, faintly green, pink and blue. The dark shapes of the skyscrapers faded into the mist which softened their too symmetrical outlines. It was indeed a fairy picture, very different from that formed in our minds by the many photographs we had seen before leaving England. We were thrilled and delighted that our arrival had taken place at this magical hour. So we set foot on American soil in a most receptive state of mind.

In view of our deep interest in food, before we had left home and when we were in the planning stage of our trip to America, we had discussed with friends who knew the country well what we were to expect in the way of entertainment during our proposed tour. No very clear pattern had emerged from these talks so we were prepared for an interesting variety of experiences.

Now follows the picture of what the European must expect in restaurants and hotels throughout the U.S.A. In private houses and clubs there are great contrasts. Rapid City provided us with a vivid experience of the great hospitality that the foreigner will meet. Our hostess, whom we had met for the first time that day, had taken immense pains to prepare a luxurious lunch. Many hours must have gone into the fabrication of the main dish which was presented with great skill. But in it were so many warring tastes that the result, to a European palate, was quite unsatisfactory. On the whole the 'West' disappointed us in this way. Great exceptions there were.

In a women's club in Oregon we were served with a most delicious shrimp dish cooked in a sauce that I longed to mop up with a spoon or piece of bread, *à la française*. Here too we met that excellent herb called Oregano. At Colorado Springs the college faculty treated us to a lamb chop that was a gastronome's heaven. The chop was boned and wrapped round a kidney. Round the chop was bound a rasher of bacon. Slightly conflicting tastes perhaps, but so good!

On the air lines we used the food was quite pleasant and 'United' produced a minute steak that was excellent. On trains, however, the standard ranged from moderate to low, considering the prices charged.

During our bus rides, usually starting at the unearthly hour of 6 a.m., we ate at luncheonettes. In these the food was simple and well cooked, while the coffee varied from good to excellent. The prices were commendably low, and we enjoyed the variety of newly-baked bread that was almost universally available. This is a very good point. In many of the hotels at which we stayed a wide selection of wheaten and corn breads is carried round the dining-tables in a heated aluminium container from which the guests can make their choice. This is a system which should be copied in Europe and particularly in Britain, where as a rule only

41

a very dull white or brown bread, baked at least twenty-four hours earlier, is available with a meal.

As we worked our way from north to south, to New Orleans and Palm Beach, we became excited at the thought of testing and tasting the southern cooking. So much had been told us of the specialities that we should find in New Orleans that we could hardly wait. But life is full of disappointments. My wife pronounced oysters cooked with a special spinach dressing as acceptable and interesting and I had one good dish, a *Riz de veau financière*, no better and no worse than could be found in a good European restaurant. Gumbo soup had no message for either of us. We had heard so much about it, only to find it was very much like any other *purée* concocted from dried beans, and equally dull.

Palm Beach held no surprises. The entertainment offered was that of any big European sea-side resort, while in private houses, as in New Orleans, the level was that of similar establishments in France.

On then to Georgia and the lovely town of Savannah, where English influence is visible in its azalea-lined avenues and tree-filled squares, designed by the British General Oglethorpe. Our hotel was pleasant but followed the American convention in matters of food and drink. We lunched later in the Oglethorpe club and suffered the ordeal of a preliminary drinking session. But the meal made up for it all. Starting with sticks of the perfect American celery, a vegetable that profits from refrigeration, we went on to a delicious shrimp soup with a cream basis. A plain grilled steak followed, crisped and burned at the edges and tender as a maiden's love. With it was served a lettuce salad that should have been excellent but, like a fool, I took a dressing without prior investigation. It was filled with strong Roquefort cheese! This was the only blot on a perfect meal, and my own fault.

Dinner at the same place was equally good. The outstanding dish was a prawn curry—a real curry, full of herbs, fresh and pungent. Amazingly a sparkling Burgundy was served throughout the meal. This is a wine that I despise, but for some reason which I find obscure it went reasonably well. Perhaps my palate was becoming inured to shocks.

No Icebergs in My Glass

In Wilmington, North Carolina, there was the same contrast between refined cooking in private houses and the usual unappetizing meals in the local hotels. We had arrived late owing to trouble with our aeroplane and our hosts had almost given us up. However the programme went through in the end and the next day our hosts insisted on giving us lunch before our departure for New York.

Although we were due to take off at one o'clock, we were still drinking cocktails at twenty past twelve! In the result a superb fish soup, a finely roasted chicken and an ambrosial wine jelly and syllabub had to be bolted in a matter of minutes. We got into our seats with a few seconds to spare, our tummies complaining bitterly that they had no time to enjoy or digest a magnificent meal. At least the aircraft did not fail us this time and we got safely to New York.

So far I have made only a glancing reference to the drinking habits in the States. Let me say at once that I believe America to be more sober than Europe. Taking the country as a whole it looks as though less alcohol is drunk than by Europeans. The Mormon influence, the women's temperance associations and the strain of business life conspire to keep the American from alcoholism. At the same time he is robbed by custom of one of the real joys of life, the drinking of good wine with good food. It may be argued that the quantity of alcohol absorbed in the drinking sessions before a meal is excessive, and if it was set against the amount drunk in a glass of sherry and a bottle of wine at table the European might emerge as the more sober. But because more Europeans drink alcoholic liquors than Americans my first statement is not unfair. By comparison, however, who gets the greater satisfaction? After the drinking session often an American meal begins with icebergs in a glass of water that additionally is so chlorinated as to smell like a gas attack in the Kaiser's War. It continues with coffee served with the meat course. This is a conflicting taste, alien and repellent to the European palate. Smoking throughout a meal is very prevalent and I think it is a disgusting habit.

Americans will say that much of my criticism of their national cooking can justifiably be applied to the average British meal. I admit at once that the food served in our provincial hotels and on our railways is often quite atrocious. In France the standard has fallen sharply in recent years. But in both countries the meals in many quite modest hotels and in private houses are better than in similar places in America. Having regard to the perfection of other aspects of life in the U.S.A. this is unfortunate and should be put right.

It is not necessary to be extravagant to eat and drink well. The complicated messes with which we have been served in the U.S.A. are at least as expensive, if not more so, than the plainer dishes served in Europe. Californian wine is good and cheap and in some ways preferable to imported vintages. The trouble lies in the serving. I have had to drink iced Burgundy tasting of varnish; good wines had been given me well chilled and opened at the table so that they had had no time to breathe and show their bouquet. In a New York restaurant a sound claret was so shaken up during its passage from the cellar to the table that it was cloudy and undrinkable—an elementary mistake.

It is perfectly true that many Americans have the right ideas about food and drink but very many more have not. Until this multitude have learned by travel and experience how to avoid the baser errors of the table they will not have acquired the true art of living. So for the present that deplorable triumvirate, 'Scotch on the Rocks', icebergs in chlorine water, and tomato ketchup reign supreme at the American board. It is so sad!

It is against the over-chilling of drinks that I make my principal attack. When the tongue is numbed by cold, the taste buds fail to do their work—which is to savour the dishes. Small wonder then that the food has to be highly spiced to evoke even a modest response from the palate, and that indigestion and ulcers are national diseases! Further, the American preoccupation with hygiene leads to the very extensive use of refrigeration and pasteurization as a preventive of possible infections. For example, the American oyster, frozen and dead, comes to table so tasteless that it is almost uneatable raw. I have tried some, as in England, and they might have been composed of flannel for all the pleasure

44

they gave my tongue. The British and French prefer their oysters alive, taking the risk of catching typhoid in the hope that the sanitary authorities will have seen to it that no sewage gets into the oyster beds. In my opinion there is no better flavour than that of the Colchester 'native' or Helford river oyster, not twenty-four hours out of the sea, and opened before one at the bar of Wilton's or Cunningham's in London's West End. Dead and frozen they would also taste of wet flannel. The American fear of tubercular and other infections has led to many other foods being passed through the equivalent of a chemical laboratory before they are offered for sale. Consequently, unless treated with strong sauces, they are completely flavourless. This was the main cause of our disappointment with American food. There were other troubles too.

The size of the portions served in the U.S.A. and their presentation shocks the European. While admitting that before 1914 it was commonplace in a French restaurant to order one portion for two persons who would feel well satisfied with this amount, these days are gone. In England the baron of beef and indeed the humbler sirloin have almost disappeared. But in the U.S.A. a single steak will overlap the edges of a big dinner-plate. To make matters worse it is served with a mound of vegetables and other trimmings. More than half is wasted, even by Americans, who are still notable trenchermen. The European loses his appetite at the sight of the formidable task confronting him.

Certain basic similarities do exist in the art of cooking and these are to be found where, in the big cities such as New York, Paris, Rome and London, there is an accepted international technique. But whether there are similarities or not it is the quality of the material, meat, fish, game and poultry, that exercises the greatest influence on national food forms. Where, owing to poor grazing, scrub stock or lack of rainfall the material is poor, then hot sauces and strong spices are needed to make the dishes palatable. Where the material is good then the food is prepared simply. This is the normal state of affairs but America, as we were to discover in our journeyings through the majority of the states of the Union, is exceptional.

No Icebergs in My Glass

In spite of the fact that the quality of the meat and vegetables available in the U.S.A. is of a very high order, there is a general tendency to ruin them by the use of highly seasoned sauces and accompanying side dishes which introduce four or five warring flavours. When a French or other continental chef prepares a sauce and vegetables to go with meat he is most careful to blend all the tastes so that they do not quarrel but form a single appetizing whole. In America we have been served with several sauces, each different in character, and with vegetables smothered in dressings in which a strong-tasting cheese such as Roquefort kills any finesse. Iced water and black coffee served at the same time have completed the destruction of any desire to eat. I am convinced that one of the reasons for this gastronomical atrocity lies in the average American's approach to food. It seems to be the custom to invite guests to arrive anything from an hour to two hours before a meal is to be served. During that time very cold drinks such as 'Scotch on the Rocks' are served in quantity. There are indeed icebergs in the glass, and the ration of spirit is most generous. As a result, as I have already said, the taste buds on the tongue are frozen and drugged into insensibility.

It is the intrusion of this form of eating and drinking into our accepted technique in Britain and on the Continent of Europe that I find most distressing. Before long we shall be following the American pattern and indigestion, nerves and ulcers will be common form. We shall chatter like apes over our fifth dry Martini or sixth 'Scotch' and then sit down to a meal that will burn holes in our insides.

Glad I am to have known the great days of dining-room culture, and still to be able to cling to the vestiges of a past civilization in my kitchen and on my table.

So much then for my philosophy on food and drink. Now to the practical side of this important business. I am reserving for my closing chapter a few notes concerning vegetable cookery, but a brief note on wines follows immediately.

CHAPTER VII

On Drinking at Meals

In previous chapters I have indicated the kind of drink that I like to take with my meals, but here again personal preference must play a great part. There is also the important point that some people cannot swallow certain types of drink without suffering in consequence. For example, it is many years since I was able to drink whisky regularly. Now I must limit myself to the occasional tot. In general, however, there are certain rules which, if followed, will give that great satisfaction—the drinking of a liquid which is right for the food being eaten. How sorry I am for those who for one reason or another do not drink with their meals. They forfeit one of the great pleasures of life.

I suppose the broad rule is to drink red wine with most roasts and substantial meat dishes, and white with fish, and white meats, also with certain small game (though not for all tastes). The type of red or white depends very largely on the way the meat or fish is prepared. Lightly flavoured dishes are best accompanied by the better wines, whose bouquet is not destroyed by too much seasoning in the dish. Strongly flavoured dishes call for rough wines, such as Portuguese or Spanish reds, or indeed a can of beer, which is the most suitable accompaniment to curry.

Sweets are best partnered with a sweetish white wine such as a

On Drinking at Meals

Château Yquem, not necessarily a 'Grand Cru', which is double the price of, say, a Flora Blanche sauterne. Cheese and fruit go well with port.

On this matter of port there are two schools of thought. Some people say that one should never smoke while drinking port—either vintage or light. This is something of a fallacy. If I was offered a Taylor 1927—a most exquisite wine—I should not smoke till I had drunk my fill. But with light port, tobacco does no harm. However, if anyone at my table smoked while drinking an Ausone claret of 1934 he would never darken my doors again. So, no smoking with good claret, but no particular harm with port.

Some people (not I) nowadays will drink Barsac right through a meal; others think this effeminate. At 16s. or 17s. a bottle, it is said to be gaining in popularity all the time. *Vin rosé* is a versatile wine which, in a sense, overlaps the reds and whites and can be drunk with many different dishes.

To illustrate these points I give two menus such as I would select to give pleasure to my friends.

Grilled sole	Amontillado Sherry
Roast duck	Cheval Blanc 1947
Stilton cheese and celery	Vintage port according to availability

Potage Germiny	Meursault
Grilled rump steak with onions	Campo Grande (Portuguese Burgundy type)
Cox's orange pippins	Non-vintage port

Considerable ingenuity can be employed when preparing a menu. I remember a dinner I ate in a friend's house during the days of rationing:

Turtle soup	Madeira *circa* 1824
Grilled sole	Batard-Montrachet 1934
Roast pheasant	Mouton-Rothschild 1929
Comice pear	Château Yquem
Cox's apple	Dow's 1927

It will be noted that this five-course dinner in no way broke the regulations!

On Drinking at Meals

Go to your local wine merchant and find out what he has got, having previously read one or two books such as *Wine and the Wine Lands of the World*, or George Bijur's *Wines with Long Noses*. Wine is worth a study, but don't try to show off to a wine merchant. He will blind you with his science. Since I have said that a taste for wine is a very personal thing, try your tongue on clarets white and red, burgundies of both colours, Spanish reds —their whites are a closed book to me—and Portuguese reds which are really quite good. From Yugoslavia come excellent whites which are as good as the Alsatian Rieslings and Traminers, and are about thirty per cent cheaper. But remember that on the whole price is a good indication of quality. Don't waste your time on Cypriot or Greek wines or anything that comes from the Americas. California produces fair wines at great expense. Peruvian wines taste of stone.

Brandy or liqueurs with which to finish a meal are a problem nowadays. All are very expensive—none as good as they were. I suppose the safest bet is V.S.O.P. brandy from one of the good 'names'. Personally I prefer Hine. I am not a champagne drinker. I don't like it at a meal, and I particularly dislike the French habit of serving it after white and red wines have been drunk with the earlier courses.

To sum up: try to blend the drinks with the food—delicate wines with delicate dishes, strong rough wines with highly flavoured concoctions; white with white and red with red; and above all do not numb your taste buds with large quantities of very cold alcohol.

CHAPTER VIII

On Short Drinks

It is many years since the habit of taking a short drink as an appetizer became normal in Britain. Sherry at first, and then cocktails, came into common usage as an introduction to dinner. The taking of a glass of light port with a slice of plum cake at 11 a.m. followed closely the Frenchman's *apéritif* habit, and was current some time before the cocktail era.

There are many hundreds of cocktails, some of them so stickily sweet as to spoil the appetite rather than excite it. Gin is the basis of most of them and the best of them, in my opinion, is the Martini. This should be made in the proportion of five parts gin to one of vermouth, stirred round with a strip of fresh lemon-peel and ice. Purists forbid shaking and use a wooden spoon for stirring.

Of the more exotic cocktails the Daisy is very good. An Arab bar-tender in Switzerland taught me how to make it: In a champagne glass place a lump of sugar soaked with Angostura bitters. Add a few drops of cherry brandy and brandy. Fill the glass a third full with crushed ice and pour on enough champagne almost to fill the glass. Top with a slice of fresh orange. This drink is guaranteed to banish fatigue or depression.

It is not advisable to drink a heavy brown sherry before a meal.

On Short Drinks

Eleven a.m. is the time for this. Stick to Tio Pepe or Army & Navy No. 30, but if these are too dry, then any light sherry is appropriate. Short drinks should be served not more than half an hour before the meal, otherwise their effect is to numb the appetite rather than enhance it, especially if they are served too frequently and very cold. Incidentally, too much liquid before a meal dilutes the gastric juices and thus promotes indigestion and ulcers!

CHAPTER IX

The Kitchen and its Equipment

Success in cooking depends to a considerable extent on the lay-out of the kitchen and the possession of the right equipment.

Very large sums of money can be spent on the kitchen if professionals are commissioned to establish it according to the ideas of modern domestic equipment designers. It certainly is very nice to have the room lined with two-toned cupboards, with a stainless steel sink, teak draining-boards, mobile refrigerators and washing-machines, garbage destructors, expensive mixers and so forth. But the ordinary individual can manage very nicely if he sticks to certain principles.

The key to the whole business is, of course, the position of the stove. It must be accessible and in a strong light. Everything else should turn round this point.

In my own kitchen the stove is only four feet from a big window with a north-east light. Immediately above it and at eye-level is the spit roaster—a Cannon. Both stove and roaster are heated by gas. I am quite hopeless with an electric stove unless it is one of the American monstrosities that has as many stops as a cinema organ. Only on such a machine can I control my simmering and gentle stewing. On any other electric stove my percentage

The Kitchen and its Equipment

of carbonized food is very high. If I cannot have gas I will manage with an Aga, supplemented by a small electric stove for quick work.

To the immediate left of the stove, but well insulated from it, is the grocery cupboard where are kept the herbs and flavourings. On a shelf above are flour, sugar, raisins, pepper and salt. To the right the wall is covered with peg-board on which hang the pots and pans and knives. Below is the Formica preparing board under which is a drawer containing the slices, the kitchen table-knives, forks and spoons. At right angles runs the draining-board, the sink and the second draining-board. The rest of the kitchen walls are cupboarded, except where the refrigerator has its being. The washing-machine lives under the left-hand draining-board and the gas water heater under that on the right. Under the sink there is the usual assortment of buckets and cleaning materials.

The whole point about this layout is that things in regular use are visible and within arm's length. Two paces from the stove brings everything needed under my hand. This general arrangement has enormously increased the convenience and speed with which the cooking can be carried out.

As regards utensils there are two of every useful size of saucepan, except the one big fish kettle. There are some dozen knives, small, medium and large. Of specialist tools there are:

(1) the Cannon cooker which does everything but talk,
(2) The Paladin mixer, which grinds the coffee every morning, mixes the soups and makes the *mousses*,
(3) the pressure cooker for reducing bones and carcasses to stock and fat,
(4) several kinds of slicer to save the cutting-up jobs,
(5) a clockwork timer.

Of course there must be many other successful arrangements, but I am convinced that they are established around the stove which itself imposes accessibility and a good light as essential features of its position in the kitchen.

Finally, there is the question of cooking smells. Ideally the kitchen should be by itself at the top of the house with very rapid communications with the dining-room. This arrangement is seldom possible in a house and never in a flat. I solved the problem, when designing a house many years ago, by insulating the kitchen from the dining-room, at one end with the butler's pantry and at the other by double doors. In my present flat a door that closes tightly and a good extractor fan in the kitchen window reduce the problem to manageable proportions.

Now let us consider the actual preparation of the food we are going to eat. As an Englishman of French origin, I begin, very naturally, with sauces.

CHAPTER X

Sauces

We English are frequently accused by the French of being a nation of eighty religions and one sauce. To a Frenchman any dish is incomplete unless it has a sauce which he can mop up with a piece of bread in his fingers, which he then pops into his mouth. This act, slightly non-U to our eyes, is almost a religious observance. It is certainly intended as a compliment by a guest to his hostess.

This criticism by the French is still valid. Basically we use gravies (which are not sauces) or that great stand-by, the white sauce, *roux* or *béchamel*. Composed of butter, flour, stock or milk the *roux* is the handiest of additions to a dish. It can be given a multiplicity of flavours, cheese, tomato, mushroom, onion—the lot. Once the simple technique of making it is understood, it cannot go wrong. But what may fairly be called French sauces are a different proposition altogether and it is in the making of them that skill, care and patience are required.

These sauces seem to me to fall into two main categories; those suitable for eggs, fish and vegetables and those that go with game and meat. In the latter wine can be used with considerable advantage, but not always in the former. Fish is the occasional exception.

The prime sauce of the first category is undoubtedly *mayonnaise*.

55

Sauces

It has a dozen uses and, if certain simple directions are closely followed, is easy to make. A *mayonnaise* contains yolk of egg, oil, salt and either lemon juice or vinegar. I prefer the lemon juice.

Having carefully cleared the white from the yolk, place the latter in a *warmed* bowl. Then add small quantities of oil heated to 70° F., beating the mixture all the while. In two or three minutes it will thicken and then each dose of oil can be increased. When the sauce is in sufficient quantity and clings thickly to the beater, add the lemon juice and salt to taste.

Some cook-books speak of making the sauce from cold ingredients. This is a basic error and the cause of much frustration. The temperature of the oil (70° F.) is critical. If too hot the egg might start cooking and if too cold the sauce will not thicken without an infinity of labour. I keep my oil (nut oil for preference) in a cupboard over the hot water cylinder and its temperature is always just right.

My next sauce is a *hollandaise*. This is more elaborate, and not so easy to make, but it is excellent with fish and asparagus.

Egg-yolks, butter, lemon juice, salt and pepper are the ingredients. To fill a large sauce-boat, three eggs, ¼ lb. best butter, a coffee-spoon of salt, a dash of white pepper, three soup-spoons of vinegar and a dessertspoonful of lemon juice are needed.

Clear the whites from the yolks as thoroughly as possible, and place the latter in a bowl. Then take a small saucepan, deep and narrow with a thick base, or a double saucepan. This type of pan will help to prevent the sauce cooking too fiercely. In the saucepan put the vinegar, salt and pepper and two soup-spoons of water. Bring to the boil and let it boil until the liquid is reduced to about a soup-spoonful. Remove from the stove to cool, and add a little cold water.

Meanwhile you have been dicing the butter into lumps as big as a hazel nut.

To the reduced vinegar add the eggs, and beat briskly. Then put in about an ounce of butter and return the saucepan to a very gentle heat. Keep stirring as the butter melts and add single lumps as soon as the sauce begins to thicken. Always keep some cold

56

water handy to add if the sauce thickens too quickly. This thickening, if it occurs, is due to the eggs cooking too rapidly.

When all the butter has been incorporated in the sauce take the saucepan off the fire and add the lemon juice, checking for seasoning at the same time.

Sometimes the sauce will go wrong; the butter will begin to separate out and the eggs to curdle. If this happens, whip the saucepan off the fire and add a tablespoonful of very cold water. Beat briskly until the sauce regains its normal smooth aspect.

In the worst case of failure the situation can be saved by pouring the mixture into a bowl and then putting a fresh yolk into a cold saucepan. Add the mixture drop by drop to the saucepan, beating all the time. When the situation is restored, replace the saucepan on gentle heat and stir until ready.

The famous sauce *mousseline* is no more than a *hollandaise* to which two soup-spoonsful of thick cream, well beaten up, have been added at the last moment and folded in. But it is so good!

In a well-known French cookery book of which the fourteen hundred pages have been my stand-by for years, there are fifty-seven recipes for making sauces. Many of these are manifestly outside the scope of the amateur cook who cannot afford the time and trouble necessary to make them successfully. Below will be found recipes for the sauces which can most usefully and pleasantly be added to meat in its various forms.

First, a simple one—*Sauce Italienne*. This is composed of mushrooms, onions or shallots, preferably the latter, veal or beef stock, half a wineglassful of white wine or dry vermouth, tomato *purée*, butter and flour. Some experts add a little chopped lean ham and parsley, but this is not essential.

Lightly cook the onions or shallots in a small thick-bottomed saucepan. Add the mushrooms which have been chopped small. (Mushroom peelings and stalks are perfectly adequate.) Add pepper and salt and cook on a brisk flame. When all the moisture from the mushrooms has steamed off add the white wine. Allow the liquor to reduce almost completely and then add the tomato *purée* and stock. Once the mixture has boiled, turn down the flame and allow to simmer for ten minutes. Just before serving add the butter and flour in the form of a *roux*. To make enough sauce for four people you will require:

2 oz. of mushrooms or mushroom peelings
4 shallots or a medium-sized onion
2 oz. of butter
½ wineglass of white wine or vermouth
⅓ pint veal or beef stock
Heaped teaspoonful of tomato purée
2 tablespoonsful of flour

The *Sauce Duxelles* is composed essentially as above, but with a clove of garlic, chopped or pressed, for those who like the taste.

Now for some wine sauces. It seems to be a generally accepted principle, with which I agree, that only dry wines should be used for sauce-making or for the steeping (*marinage*) of meat and fish. Hence clarets, white and red, and the dry vermouths are recommended.

The lazy way of setting about making a wine sauce is to prepare your meat or fish some four hours before eating, placing it in a dish and covering it with wine in which are infused flavourings such as herbs and partly cooked shallots. At the desired time the dish is placed in the oven, covered with greaseproof paper or aluminium foil, and allowed to cook for the period necessary to bring the meat or fish almost to readiness. Then prepare a *roux* into which is poured the gravy from the dish. Mix up the ingredients and then pour on to the dish which then can be reheated under the grill for two or three minutes.

Below, however, is given the recipe for a sauce-boat of real *Sauce Bordelaise*.

The base is a brown sauce to which is added:

2 oz. butter
2 oz. chopped carrots
2 oz. chopped onions
Pinch of parsley, thyme, a leaf of bay

This should be simmered for a good half-hour. Boil together until the liquor is reduced to one-third:

3 *oz. chopped shallots*
½ *pint of a good 'table' claret*
A pinch of white pepper, of thyme, and a small bay leaf.

Mix the two sauces together, and simmer for fifteen minutes, clearing off any scum that forms. Then pass through a fine sieve and just before serving add an ounce of butter and lightly cooked diced beef marrow.

SAUCE PIQUANTE

4 *oz. onions*
4 *oz. shallots*
2 *wineglassfuls of vinegar*
½ *pint meat stock*
3 *oz. butter*
3 *oz. flour*
4 *oz. chopped gherkins*
4 *oz. capers*
Chopped parsley, chervil and tarragon

First boil the finely chopped onions and shallots with the vinegar in a small saucepan until the liquid is reduced by half. Then add the stock and boil for three minutes. Pour the contents of the saucepan into a bowl, clean and dry the saucepan and in it make a *roux*. Add the liquid from the bowl and bring to the boil. Take it off the flame and allow to simmer for fifteen minutes, keeping the surface clear of fat and scum. Just before serving see that there is enough salt and then add pepper, gherkins, capers and the herbs.

SAUCE VINAIGRETTE

I give rather a complicated recipe for this sauce. It can be simplified by omitting the pimento and cucumber pickle.

1 *tablespoon dried pimento*
1 *tablespoon cucumber pickle*
¾ *tablespoon green pepper—chopped fine*
3 *sprigs parsley*
1 *small onion chopped or chives*
3 *tablespoons vinegar*
3 *tablespoons oil*

Sauces

First cook the vinegar and oil and when hot add the other ingredients finely chopped.

Mix well, using a double boiler to prevent burning. Serve either hot or cold.

SAUCE MORNAY

The basis of this sauce is a thin *roux* (*béchamel*) to which is added grated Gruyère cheese mixed with Parmesan, in equal proportions. Choose your Gruyère dry, as otherwise it becomes rather like glue when cooked. Heat the *roux* in a saucepan, add the cheese, stirring until it is melted. Remove from the flame and add about 1 oz. of butter in small pats, stirring all the time. When the liaison is complete the sauce is ready. *Sauce Mornay*, when used with fish, is the better for a proportion of fish stock in the *roux*.

In general use the addition of cream to the *roux* improves the flavour—and adds to the cost!

DELHI SAUCE

7 *lb. ripe tomatoes, skinned and cleaned*
2 *lb. sugar*
4 *oz. salt*
1 *quart malt vinegar*
2 *lb. raisins*
4 *oz. garlic*
4 *oz. root ginger* } *pounded and ground up together*
1 *oz. red chillies*

This is a most excellent sauce to make when tomatoes are cheap. It goes with curry and indeed with any highly flavoured dish. A by-product of the sauce is an excellent chutney.

Boil together in a large saucepan, and then allow to simmer gently for at least an hour. Strain off the liquid and bottle as the sauce. The solid matter forms the chutney.

CURRY SAUCE

This is a very simple sauce.

1 *tablespoon curry powder*
1 *small onion or 3 shallots—chopped*
1 *oz. butter; garlic salt, stock.*

60

Soften the onions in the butter, add the curry powder, garlic salt and stock. Cover and simmer for half an hour, adding more stock as necessary.

APPLE SAUCE

2 *cooking apples*
2 *tablespoons sugar*
2 *cloves*

Core and peel the apples and chop. Boil for ten minutes or until soft, adding the sugar and cloves when ready. Cook for another five minutes and pass through a sieve.

SAUCE BIGARRADE

This is finely sliced orange and lemon peel, flavoured with Cointreau, and cooked in a good stock.

TOMATO SAUCE

Tomatoes, cleaned and peeled, onions or shallots, tomato *purée*, butter, salt and pepper, cooked and crushed together and then mixed with a good meat stock.

CAPER SAUCE

This is simply a *roux* or *béchamel* to which capers have been added a few minutes before serving.

BAGNAROTTE SAUCE

1 *breakfastcup mayonnaise sauce*
2 *dessertspoons tomato ketchup*
2 *teaspoons fresh cream*
2 *coffee-spoons Worcestershire sauce*
2 *coffee-spoons brandy*
Dash tabasco, drops lemon juice, salt and pepper

SAUCE DUGLÉRÉ

Mayonnaise sauce to which a cold fish stock in which shallots, parsley and a glass of white wine have been cooked, is added.

Sauces

SAUCE BÉARNAISE

This is a *hollandaise* sauce to which has been added another sauce composed of:

1 *soup-spoon tarragon vinegar*
1 *soup-spoon white wine*
2 *chopped shallots*
Teaspoon dried tarragon
Teaspoon dried chervil
1 *egg-yolk and 2 oz. butter*

Cook this mixture very slowly in a small saucepan until the liquid is reduced to not more than two tablespoons. Rub through a sieve firmly to get the most out of the herbs. Allow to cool. When ready, begin to make the *hollandaise* sauce as already indicated, and as soon as the egg-yolks are in the saucepan add the secondary sauce. Above all things do not allow this sauce to boil. It can be served at quite a gentle heat.

SAUCE ROBERT

2 *large onions*
4 *oz. butter*
1 *tablespoon flour*
½ *pint stock or milk*
Dessertspoon mustard
Salt, pepper, two lumps sugar

Chop the onions finely and cook them slowly in the butter until they are golden brown. Then add the flour, stock, mustard, pepper and salt. Mix thoroughly with a wooden spoon and leave to simmer for a few minutes. Add more stock if the sauce thickens too quickly. Then melt the sugar in a spoonful of water, and caramelize it. This gives the sauce a good colour. This sauce can be used with veal or pork, or any oddments of meat left over.

Cumberland Sauce can be bought ready made, but if it is desired to use it freshly prepared, here is a convenient recipe.

In the proportion necessary for the dish with which the sauce is to be served dice finely orange and lemon peel. Blanch the mixture and then add to it:

Sauces

Red currant jelly thinned with white wine
Vinegar, salt and mustard
A liqueur glassful of Madeira

Proceed cautiously with the flavouring, tasting from time to time to see that all is well.

Sauce Genevoise is a very good fish sauce and can be made very simply. The ingredients are:

Finely diced onions and carrots
Flour—a small quantity only—just enough to thicken the mixture
Fish stock
Red wine

Cook the vegetables lightly in butter, stirring in the flour as they cook.

Add the fish stock and boil for a quarter of an hour.

In a saucepan reduce the red wine by half. Then add the sauce and again reduce the liquid to the desired amount. Finally add a knob of anchovy butter.

CHAPTER XI

Month-by-Month Menus

The rest of this book, apart from a few notes on potato recipes and the preparation of vegetables generally, is devoted to menus for the evening meal. These are divided by the seasons, spring, summer, autumn and winter, so that the material used is neither difficult to obtain nor wildly expensive. The dishes for each menu are given in quantities suitable for two people, the recipes are as simple as possible, and the number of pots and pans used kept down to a minimum.

Very few people today have the time or opportunity to prepare elaborate meals. Even the daily effort of feeding a hungry husband is exhausting, both mentally and physically. I have tried therefore in this book to offer a simple guide which should lighten the housewife's task.

If it is desirable to alter a menu each dish is indexed in such a way that variations can be carried out with the minimum of difficulty.

No. 1 ONION SOUP
LAMB CUTLETS
SCOTCH FLUMMERY

ONION SOUP

2 *medium-sized onions*
2 *ounces butter*
2 *tablespoons of flour*
½ *pint boiled milk*
Salt, pepper

Cut the onions finely, removing the hard core. Melt the butter in a saucepan with a thick base. This prevents the butter browning. Add the onions and stir constantly with a wooden spoon until they are a golden colour. Add the flour and keep on stirring over a low flame, until the whole mixture is golden in colour. Then add either water or stock to the required quantity and bring to the boil. Then allow to simmer for ten minutes. The boiling milk is then added. When ready to serve, pour into the soup dishes and place a slice of toast covered with grated cheese on top of the soup. Gruyère is the best cheese for the purpose, but Cheddar will do. An alternative to toast is thin slices of French bread. These should be placed at the bottom of the soup bowl and covered with the cheese. Then add the soup.

LAMB CUTLETS, POTATOES, CARROTS BOURGEOISE

The cutlets can of course be plain grilled, three to four minutes each side. But here is something a little more elaborate.

Heat butter or fat or a mixture of butter and oil. When it is hot, not boiling, place the cutlets in the pan for two minutes each side. Remove them to a plate to cool.

Break two eggs into a dish of oil, pepper and salt. Beat until the yolk and white are well mixed but not becoming frothy.

E   65

Roll the cutlets in a thin layer of flour and then plunge them into the egg mixture. Lay them aside until ten minutes before serving.

Heat the oil and butter in the pan until it begins to smoke and then cook the cutlets for three minutes each side. Finish them off for three or four minutes in the oven, but do not cover! Place them on the dish, garnish and keep hot until serving. Mashed potatoes go well with cutlets but alternatives can be found on page 163 (Potato Recipes).

Carottes bourgeoise take about an hour to prepare. For two people three large carrots, a small onion, an ounce of butter, one tablespoon of flour, half pint of clarified stock, a gill of milk, one yolk of egg, chopped parsley, teaspoon of granulated sugar, salt and pepper.

Scrape and wash the carrots and cut them into slices of the same thickness so that they cook evenly. Cut the onion into thin slices. Place the vegetables in a thick-bottomed saucepan, add the butter, salt and sugar. Without covering allow to stew very gently, stirring from time to time to keep the bits from sticking together. After thirty minutes add the flour, stirring very carefully so as not to break up the softened vegetables. After three minutes add the pepper, stock and milk and bring to the boil, stirring constantly. As soon as the mixture has boiled, place it on a very low flame and allow to simmer for fifteen minutes.

Shortly before serving fold in the yolk of egg, place on the dish and scatter the chopped parsley over the vegetables.

SCOTCH FLUMMERY

⅓ *pint double cream*
¼ *lb. honey*
Coffee-spoon lemon juice
2 *dessertspoons whisky*

Beat the cream until fairly thick; add the honey, lemon and whisky. Put into individual dishes and sprinkle with raw oatmeal.

January

No. 2 Hors-d'œuvre
Beef Casserole
Bananes Flambées

HORS-D'ŒUVRE

Sardines
Hard-boiled eggs with mayonnaise *sauce*
Sliced tomatoes with French dressing
Pickled red cabbage

BEEF CASSEROLE

¾ *lb. good leg beef*
1 *small parsnip*
2 *small onions*
4 *small mushrooms*
4 *carrots*
½ *pint beef or veal stock*
Salt, pepper and a pinch of origanum herbs

Cut the beef up into dice about ¾-inch square, taking care to remove gristle and any excess fat. Roll the dice in flour, clean the vegetables and cut them up small. Do not skin the mushrooms—it is quite unnecessary and the stems can be used as well. Place in a suitable casserole, add the stock and seasoning and put to simmer for at least three hours. Shortly before serving, say ten or fifteen minutes before, add two tablespoons of burgundy or claret.

BANANES FLAMBÉES

Bananes flambées are prepared as follows:
Melt in a baking-dish three tablespoons butter. In it place six peeled bananas, taking care they are not brown or over-ripe. Sprinkle them with three tablespoons of brown sugar, and add one tablespoon of lemon juice. Bake uncovered in a moderate oven until tender, turning them occasionally. Add a wineglassful of rum and when ready to serve heat a tablespoon of rum until it flames and pour over the dish. Serve at once.

No. 3 Madrilène

Kedgeree and curry sauce

Crepes à la mode de Champgault

MADRILÈNE

A *madrilène* soup sounds easy to prepare but to get the best results care must be used.

In a bowl crush six fresh tomatoes. Pass the pulp through a fine sieve. Add a dessertspoon of tomato *purée*. Take four breakfast-cups of good meat stock, preferably chicken, well clarified. Put the whole into a saucepan with a small bundle of herbs done up in muslin—a clove of garlic, pinch of parsley, thyme or mint. Simmer for not less than thirty minutes, test for flavouring, add salt and pepper to taste.

KEDGEREE

The basis of a good kedgeree is fresh haddock, but any other white fish will do.

Boil ¾ lb. fresh haddock for fifteen minutes and at the same time hard-boil two eggs. Chop the eggs finely and incorporate with the fish in a bowl. Add enough milk to keep the mixture moist, and season with salt and pepper. Meanwhile your rice has been boiling with a leaf of bay for fifteen minutes in salt water. Strain into a colander, wash under the hot tap, and put in the oven to dry. Place the fish in a well-buttered open dish. The rice is then put on top with three or four good pats of butter resting on it. Cover with foil or greaseproof paper and heat in the oven at 3 while you are preparing the curry sauce, which is simply ½ oz. of melted butter, two tablespoons of curry powder, a dash of garlic salt and a little milk. Serve separately.

CRÊPES CHAMPGAULT

This dish consists of pancakes filled with a rich mixture of fruit pulp or jam and red wine or brandy.

Place four tablespoons of flour in a bowl. Make a 'well' in the centre and crack two eggs into it. Stir with the addition of milk and salt until a smooth batter is formed. Now beat well for ten minutes, adding milk to get the required consistency, cover and leave for an hour.

During this time prepare your filling. This can be made from fresh crushed fruit of whatever colour you fancy or from seedless jam. For half a dozen pancakes take two tablespoons of the fruit, add a tablespoon of brandy or red wine, thicken the mixture with caster sugar, and leave to stand.

Cooking pancakes successfully requires skill and experience, but one of the simpler methods is that devised by a Bretonne cook 130 years ago. The prepared batter is cooked in a small saucepan without any addition whatsoever. Heat your saucepan to a moderate temperature. Pour in a spoonful of the batter and tilt the pan so that the mixture covers the whole bottom. Run a knife round the edges to prevent the batter sticking. If you do not care to toss your pancake, turn it over with a slice. When ready place on a plate to keep warm. The pan will probably be quite hot enough to cook the second pancake, and it is essential never to get the pan too hot. There trouble lies!

When the pancakes are ready spread the filling and then fold. Dust with caster or icing sugar, heap into a pile and serve. The advantage of this method of cooking is that the pancakes are light, dry and easily digestible.

No. 4 ŒUFS FLORENTINES
SHOULDER OF LAMB
LEMON WHIP

ŒUFS FLORENTINES

Poached eggs on spinach with a cheese sauce. The sauce is simply a *roux* into which grated cheese, salt, pepper and celery salt have been incorporated. Celery salt brings out the cheese flavour.

SHOULDER OF MUTTON

A shoulder can be on the big side for two people. Cut off the leg end, bone it and roll it. Rub with salt and garlic salt and roast for the usual twenty minutes per pound at Regulo 5. Put the potatoes parboiled into the baking-tin so that they roast at the same time.

If it is preferred to roast the whole shoulder carry out the necessary 'salting' and cook for the normal period but, if anything, on the short side. The cold mutton you will be eating next day is much more agreeable if it is very slightly underdone and moist.

LEMON WHIP

3 eggs
1 dessertspoon powdered gelatine
1 tablespoon cold water
5 or 6 tablespoons caster sugar
Finely grated rind of 1 lemon
5 tablespoons lemon juice
2 tablespoons hot water

Separate yolk from white, soak gelatine in cold water, beat egg-yolks and sugar until light and creamy, add lemon rind and juice. Pour hot water on gelatine, stir until dissolved, add to egg mixture, mix thoroughly, now whip the egg-white until quite stiff, fold into lemon mixture; continue with a gentle up and down folding movement until you have mixed in all the white. Turn into a bowl to set.

No. 5　GRILLED GRAPE FRUIT
BOILED FOWL
RICE, ONIONS OR SHALLOTS, CARROTS
HADDOCK CANAPÉS

GRAPE FRUIT

Grilled grape fruit is a pleasant change from the cold variety.

Prepare your grape fruit in the ordinary way, and cover with brown sugar. Place under the grill until heated through, the sugar beginning to melt and the edge of the skin turning brown.

70

January

BOILED FOWL

Boiled fowl sounds dull, but can be very palatable if care is taken in the preparation and presentation.

Choose a youngish bird, not too old and tough and not too fat. In addition you will need:

A slice of gammon large enough to lard the bird's breast
6 oz. of carrots
4 oz. of onion
A stick of celery
A sprig of parsley
2 wine glasses of white dry wine—a Bordeaux for preference
A few strips of bacon—the trimmings off the gammon will do
1 oz butter
4 oz. mushrooms

Place the butter, bacon strips, carrots cut into thin slices, the onions cut into quarters, the celery, the parsley and the giblets together in a saucepan big enough to take the bird.

Heat on a very small flame, adding a spoonful of water from time to time. The vegetables should be soft after thirty minutes. Then add just enough water to cover them completely and continue to simmer for five minutes.

The chicken, trussed and larded, is then put in the saucepan, on its back. Add the wine and enough warm water to just cover it. Bring to the boil on a low flame, skimming the liquid from time to time. Add the mushroom peelings, a clove and salt to taste. Put the lid on the saucepan, leaving a small aperture to allow it to steam, and simmer for fifty minutes. Do not let it boil!

The Sauce. When the fowl is cooked, drain off the gravy and leave the bird in the saucepan to keep warm. In a separate saucepan make a *roux*, using the gravy as your liquid. The peeled mushrooms will have been blanching while the bird was boiling, and the liquid from them can be added to the sauce, which should now be allowed to cook very gently for about twenty minutes. Then fold in the yolks of three eggs, and a tablespoon of good cream. The rice will have been cooking at the same time. Place the bird, untrussed, on a hot dish, decorate with the mushrooms,

71

the boiled rice, and dress with part of the sauce. The remainder should be served separately in a sauce-boat.

HADDOCK CANAPÉS

A relief after the elaboration of the boiled fowl. Small fillets of smoked haddock lightly fried and served on buttered toast.

No. 6 CARROT SOUP
SOLE AU VIN BLANC
QUICHE LORRAINE

CARROT SOUP

½ *lb. carrots*
2 *small potatoes*
1½ *pints good stock*
¼ *lb. butter*
Pinch sugar
Chopped parsley

Stew the carrots in butter until they are softened. Add one pint of the stock, and the potatoes peeled and cut small. Bring to the boil, cover and leave to simmer for forty-five minutes. Pass through a sieve and return to the saucepan, adding all but a few spoons of the stock. Leave to simmer for twenty minutes, removing the scum as necessary and replacing the liquid from the stock you have reserved. Season to taste. Meanwhile prepare your *croûtons* and when ready to serve add them and the chopped parsley.

SOLE AU VIN BLANC

¾ *lb. Dover sole skinned on both sides*
1 *small onion cut into rings*
⅓ *pint white wine—either a Graves or dry vermouth*
2 *oz. butter*
1 *tablespoon flour*
2 *yolks of egg*

Place the onion rings on the bottom of a buttered dish. On

them lay the sole minus head, tail and side-bones. All of these can be stewed for stock. Add the wine, pepper and salt. Bring to the boil very gently and then place the dish in the oven, covered with greaseproof paper or foil. Allow to simmer for ten minutes. Meanwhile, with half the butter, make your *roux*, using the fish stock as the liquid. Keep it fairly thick.

When the fish is cooked, drain off the liquid through a sieve into a small bowl. Leave the dish in the oven at o to keep warm. With the liquid from this dish, thin the *roux* away from heat. Fold in the egg-yolks and bring to the boil for one minute. Remove from heat and add the rest of the butter. Test seasoning and add a squeeze of lemon juice. Pour the sauce over the fish, which should be completely covered. Serve.

QUICHE LORRAINE

¼ *pt. cream*
2 *eggs*
¼ *lb. lean bacon*
¼ *lb. mushrooms*

Line a small flan-tin with pastry. Wash, dry and slice the mushrooms finely. Cut the bacon into small dice.

Beat the eggs thoroughly with the cream and mix in the mushrooms and bacon and a pinch of pepper.

Pour the mixture into the pastry and cook for twenty-five minutes at Regulo 6.

FEBRUARY MENUS

No. 1   Consommé Rossini

Roast duck à l'anglaise

Orange salad

Comice pear au vin rouge

CONSOMMÉ ROSSINI

This is rather an expensive soup but can be quite excellent. To a basis of plain *consommé* add finely chopped truffles and very small puff pastries stuffed with *foie gras*, which are added when serving.

ROAST DUCK

Duck roasted on an open spit is to my mind greatly superior to one done in an oven. To begin with, it is much less trouble to baste and requires the minimum of watching once the correct roasting time per weight of duck has been established. There are a large number of open spit roasters on the market but that which I use is produced by Messrs. Cannon (G. A.) of Bilston, Staffs. The drive is electrical, but the heating is by gas. It is amazing how little splashing of grease takes place, and how little time, three minutes at most, is needed for cleaning the equipment after the roast has been removed. To prepare the duck, rub it well with salt, and stuff with parsley, sage and thyme, chopped and mixed with bread paste. You can count on forty-five minutes' cooking on the spit roaster. Trimmings to go with the duck can be orange salad, apple sauce or *bigarrade* (see Sauces). As vegetables I prefer peas and chip potatoes.

COMICE PEAR AU VIN ROUGE

Place the pears, unpeeled, in a pan and cover with red wine. Add sugar and a little lemon peel. Cook in the oven at moderate heat (Regulo 3) until the liquor is reduced by half.

74

No. 2   CHICKEN SOUP
      GRILLED RUMP STEAK
      SAUCE PIQUANTE
      CANAPÉ DIANE

CHICKEN SOUP

From time to time boiled chicken is on the menu. You will have saved the stock in which the chicken was boiled and there may well be bits of chicken left over on the dish. Thicken the stock with the addition of a small quantity of flour and cook gently for fifteen minutes. Meanwhile pound up the bits of chicken into a mash and add to the stock. Cook for ten more minutes. Whip three yolks of egg in one-third pint cream, and add to the stock when this has cooled down sufficiently not to start cooking the eggs. Pass through a fine sieve and serve.

GRILLED RUMP STEAK

Buy your rump steak in a piece at least ¾-inch thick. Beat it out until it is half this thickness. Dress with salt and pepper and a dash of garlic salt. Cook under a really hot grill to seal it and crisp the outside—three minutes each side.

Sauce piquante (see Sauces)

CANAPÉ DIANE

Cook some chicken livers in butter for four minutes. Wrap each portion in a slice of raw bacon and secure with a small skewer. Sprinkle lightly with breadcrumbs, cayenne pepper and add a little butter. Place under a hot grill until the bacon is cooked, and serve on toast.

No. 3   KEBABS
      RAIE AU BEURRE NOIR
      TARTE TATIN

KEBABS

3 *kidneys*
6 *large mushrooms*
4 *slices bacon*
Bay leaves

Divide and wash the kidneys. Set them aside to dry. Peel and cook the mushrooms in butter. When lightly cooked spear the kidney meat and the other ingredients alternately on the kebab daggers. Place under the grill to cook for about ten minutes.

RAIE AU BEURRE NOIR

Skate is a fish more popular abroad than in England. But when properly prepared it is excellent eating, and moreover not too expensive. Skate need keeping for two or three days after they have been caught. When quite fresh they are a bit tough.

Small skate can be cut along the backbone, big ones cross-wise. However they are bought they should be thoroughly cleaned when raw in cold water. Cut the fish before it is cooked into the required shapes and sizes. Wash again thoroughly. Place the fish in a saucepan and cover with cold water. Add to each pound of fish a dessertspoon of salt, a wineglass of vinegar, 4 oz. of onion slices, some parsley stalks, sprig of thyme and a leaf of bay. With the saucepan uncovered bring to the boil slowly. When boiling, remove from the flame, cover the saucepan and allow to simmer gently for about twenty-five minutes.

Remove from the saucepan and place on a dish-cloth. Pour the fish stock into a bowl. With the back of a knife gently scrape off the skin, top and bottom. Replace the fish in the saucepan, cover with the stock and keep hot.

Heat your butter, about 2 oz. per pound of fish, until it begins to brown. Meanwhile the fish has been removed from the saucepan, dried, salted, peppered and dressed with chopped parsley.

Pour the browned butter over the fish and serve very hot.

TARTE TATIN

2 *large cooking apples*
Butter, sugar, pastry, cream

February

In a baking-dish which has been well buttered and covered thickly with caster sugar, place layers of apple slices, until the top of the dish is just free enough to add the pastry. Sprinkle with more sugar and a generous dressing of butter.

Cover with a light flaky dough and cook for thirty minutes. When the sugar begins to liquefy and turn brown the dish is ready. With a knife loosen the crust and then 'upset' the baking-dish into the serving dish. Add whipped cream when serving.

No. 4 Scallops St. Jacques
Scrambled egg Magda
Chocolate charlotte

SCALLOPS

2 large live scallops in their shells
A shallot, butter, pepper, salt, chopped parsley
Small glass of white wine or dry vermouth
2 oz. chopped mushrooms
Teaspoon of tomato concentrate
Breadcrumbs, chopped parsley

Open the scallops, remove the beard and the small black 'pocket'. Keep the hollow part of the shell. Wash the flesh thoroughly, and dry. Place the scallops in a saucepan with the white wine and a pinch of salt. Bring gently to the boil. Reduce the flame so that the scallops simmer very gently for five minutes. Remove and dry, keeping the stock for the sauce.

In the same saucepan melt an ounce of butter and add the chopped shallot. Simmer gently for ten minutes. Add the chopped mushrooms and the parsley. On a hot flame stir the mixture until it ceases to steam. About four minutes is enough. Then add the stock, the tomato *purée* and a tablespoon of breadcrumbs. Let the mixture cook gently until it thickens. Then add the scallops. When warmed through, place in the shells, add breadcrumbs and melted butter. When ready to serve, place under the grill for two or three minutes.

SCRAMBLED EGGS MAGDA

4 eggs
1 oz. grated Gruyère cheese
Pinch mixed herbs
2 coffee-spoons of mustard

Scramble your eggs. Add the Gruyère and keep stirring over the flame until well mixed and smooth. Remove the saucepan from the heat and add the herbs and the mustard. Stir well with a wooden spoon. Serve with fried bread as decoration.

CHOCOLATE CHARLOTTE

1 dessertspoon gelatine
¼ pint boiled milk
1 oz. cooking chocolate

Dissolve the gelatine in a small cup of water and whip in the milk and chocolate. Leave to cool, and then add 1 oz. nuts—of any description.

½ pint cream
1 white of egg
1 teaspoon vanilla
Salt, sugar

Whip the cream and white of egg separately, adding a pinch of salt to the egg. Then add to the egg three tablespoons sugar and the vanilla. Fold these into the cream and then fold in the gelatine —chocolate mixture. Pour into a mould and chill thoroughly. Unmould to serve.

No. 5 PRAGUE HAM AND PICKLED PEACHES
MIXED GRILL
COMICE PEARS, SYRUP AND ICE-CREAM

PRAGUE HAM

One of the agreeable imports that were available in the 1930s was a very delicious lean and not over-salted ham from Prague. Served as a first dish, cold and with pickled peaches, it was a very pleasant start to a meal. It is possible, but difficult, to get it now, and the alternatives are *Jambon de Parme* and *Jambon de Bayonne*.

MIXED GRILL

A mixed grill can be dull or delicious according to the amount of care expended on its preparation. The principal ingredients are:

Sausages
Kidney
Lamb cutlets
Bacon
Mushrooms
Tomato

Slice and wash the kidneys carefully. Pepper and salt them and fry them lightly in butter. Sprinkle with chopped parsley. Fry the mushrooms in the same pan.

Grill the cutlets, sausages and bacon. Save the dripping from the pan, add the butter from the frying-pan and with the mixture make a thin sauce. Keep the various items warm, and then grill the tomatoes. Serve on an open dish decorated with sprigs of parsley.

PEARS IN SYRUP

The pears will probably have to come from a tin, though it is sometimes possible to get fresh comice pears from South Africa. In this case peel and boil them in well-sugared water, for about ten minutes. Allow to cool and then add the syrup, either strawberry or raspberry, and the ice-cream on top.

No. 6 PRAWN COCKTAIL
CURRY, PUPPADOMS, GRATED COCONUT
BANANA MOUSSE

The basis of a good prawn cocktail is the tomato sauce. Peel and wash the prawns, about ¼ lb. for two people. Crush two large tomatoes and add a teaspoon of tomato *purée*. Cook the tomatoes with a small, finely sliced shallot, adding salt and pepper to taste. Prepare separately a small *roux*. When the tomatoes and shallot are cooked, rub them through a sieve and add to the *roux*. Slice a few lettuce leaves and cover the bottom of the cocktail glasses. Place on them the prawns which should have been dried. Add the sauce up to the top of the glasses, powder with cayenne or pimento, chill and serve.

BEEF CURRY

½ *lb. of good leg beef*
2 *large onions*
1 *oz. dried raisins*
Mango or tomato chutney
3 *heaped tablespoons of curry powder*
4 *bay leaves*
Teaspoon of turmeric powder
Pinch of cardamom seeds
Breakfastcup of Patna-type rice
6 *puppadoms*
2 *oz. grated coconut*

In a large frying-pan place your onions, finely sliced, the raisins, the curry powder, two bay leaves and the herbs. Cover with beef stock and ½ oz. melted butter. Leave to simmer for at least half an hour, with the lid on the frying-pan. Then add about a tablespoon of the chutney and the beef chopped into small cubes. Continue to cook slowly for another half an hour, adding more stock when the mixture gets too dry. Twenty minutes before you intend to serve the dish, place the rice in boiling salt water to which two of the four bay leaves have been added.

Meanwhile, in a frying-pan, you have been heating your oil to the point where a crumb of bread tossed into it quickly turns brown. Place the puppadoms one by one in the oil, leave them for about five seconds and then remove with a fish slice to dry. Keep warm. Drain your rice, after fifteen minutes' cooking, into a colander, wash under the hot tap, and place in the oven to dry. Don't forget to put a fire-proof dish under the colander to catch the drips.

In a warmed dish first place the rice, and add the curry. Serve the puppadoms separately and don't forget the grated coconut.

BANANA MOUSSE

Here a mechanical mixer is a great help. For two people peel
four bananas. Cook them lightly in butter, and then put them
in the mixer with two tablespoons of cream and a dessertspoon
of sugar. Serve with a glacé cherry top. The perfect sweet to take
away the bite of the curry. The traditional 'after curry' sweet is,
of course, gula malacca, but I don't know how to make it. One
day I will experiment with sago, brown sugar and cream which
I imagine must be the basis of this eastern sweet.

MARCH MENUS

COLD HADDOCK MAYONNAISE
POUSSINS AU LARD
PANCAKES WITH APPLE SAUCE

COLD HADDOCK

For two people 6 oz. of fresh haddock.

Boil until soft, skin and allow to cool. Prepare your *mayonnaise* (see page 56).

Place the haddock in thin strips in an open dish, cover with the *mayonnaise*, sprinkle with cayenne or pimento pepper and serve.

POUSSINS AU LARD

For two people:

2 *small poussins*
4 *slices of streaky bacon*
A pinch of tarragon

The best way to roast *poussins* is on a spit. If only an oven is available, prepare the birds, larding them with the bacon and stuffing them with the tarragon.

Boil the offal to make the basis of the gravy. The birds should be cooked for about twenty-five minutes in a hot oven (Regulo 5) and frequently basted.

If a spit is available follow the same procedure but with a great deal less trouble and a better result.

Serve with new potatoes and peas.

PANCAKES WITH APPLE SAUCE

For two people prepare eight very thin pancakes (see page 69) flavoured with rum. Make a thick apple sauce by boiling two medium-sized cooking apples and when soft simmering them in butter with grated lemon rind and nutmeg (only a pinch of these last flavours). When the mixture is thick, spread on the pancakes, roll them into a sausage and place in a heat-proof dish. Dust with icing sugar. Place in a hot oven for the sugar to melt and glaze the pancakes. Serve with hot rum—*flambé*.

No. 2 SCAMPI EN BROCHE AU BEURRE
BRAISED HAM, SPINACH AND NEW POTATOES
CHOCOLATE MOUSSE

Scampi, Dublin Bay prawns, Jumbo prawns, *écrevisses*, call them what you will, are generally available all the year round, frozen or fresh. Fresh ones are the best for this dish, but others will do.

Peel, clean and wash the scampi. Dry them and then place on a skewer, about four scampi per skewer. If you don't have a kebab roaster, put them under the grill and baste freely with butter. When they are a golden yellow colour (in about ten minutes under a hot grill) remove, pepper with salt and chopped parsley and serve on the skewer with thin slices of brown bread and butter and a section of fresh lemon.

BRAISED HAM WITH SPINACH

For two persons, a basin full of fresh spinach, four slices of lean ham, a glass of red wine, a chopped shallot or small onion, mixed herbs.

Put your spinach to wash and stand. Place your ham in an open fire-proof dish with the chopped shallot, the herbs, the glass of red wine and a teacup full of stock. Cover and leave to simmer in a warm oven (Regulo 3) for an hour. Add stock from time to time to keep the ham moist.

Meanwhile you have been peeling the new potatoes and chopping parsley for the dressing.

Fifteen to twenty minutes before you are ready to serve, start boiling the spinach and potatoes.

Then drain the spinach thoroughly, pressing it hard to get rid

83

of the water. Turn the ham out on to a board and pour the stock into a basin. Line the fire-proof dish with the spinach, place the ham on top. Thicken the stock with a little meat essence and pour over the ham and spinach. Cover the dish with foil or greaseproof paper and reheat in the oven. Serve with the new potatoes, well buttered and sprinkled with parsley.

CHOCOLATE MOUSSE

Melt ¼ lb. unsweetened chocolate in a double boiler with a small quantity of water—about two tablespoons. Stir until the mixture is smooth, and leave to cool. Then add three yolks of egg and ½ teaspoon of vanilla extract, beating thoroughly to make sure the blending is complete. Pour into a bowl and fold in the whites of egg that have been beaten stiff. Spoon into ramequins and leave in the lower part of the refrigerator for about two hours.

No. 3 CREAM SOUP
GRILLED TROUT
POMMES MAÎTRE D'HÔTEL
APPLE FRITTERS

CREAM SOUP

1 *pint of veal stock*
2 *oz. rice flour*
2 *egg-yolks*
Small pot of fresh cream
2 *oz. butter*

Bring two-thirds of the veal stock to the boil. Place the rice flour in a bowl and with the remainder of the stock, added slowly, make a paste. Pour slowly into the boiling stock, stirring briskly to ensure the absence of lumps. Bring back to the boil, cover the saucepan and allow to simmer very gently for about fifteen minutes. Beat the egg-yolks in the bowl with the cream, and incorporate with the simmering liquid, taking care that the eggs do not cook. When the mixture is smooth bring back to the boil for a minute. Remove from the stove and stir in the butter, divided into small lumps. Rub the soup through a fine sieve and then serve.

GRILLED TROUT

Fresh trout should be available by the middle of March. Choose two of about 8 oz. weight, split, clean and wash thoroughly. Grill under a brisk heat for about six minutes each side. Dress with butter and some chopped parsley and serve with a section of fresh lemon.

For potatoes, see Potato recipes, *Pommes maître d'hôtel*, page 164.

APPLE FRITTERS

Two medium cooking apples
Batter (prepare this two hours ahead)
Rum
Sugar

Peel, core and slice the apples into rings about ¼-inch thick, sprinkle them with the rum and sugar. Heat about ½-inch deep of maize oil in a large frying-pan, until a crumb of bread thrown into it browns in a few seconds. Dip the apple slices in the batter, coating them well on each side, and then drop in the hot oil. Turn over so that both sides become a golden brown. Remove and drain, sprinkle with sugar and serve.

No. 4 SALMON MOUSSE
LEG OF LAMB DUXELLES
RUM GÂTEAU

SALMON MOUSSE

Fresh salmon is now on the market—but usually very expensive.

Buy heads and tails in sufficient quantity to give about 4 oz. of flesh. You must judge this by eye.

1 *tablespoon sherry*
1 *tablespoon Parmesan cheese, grated*
½ *gill of thick cream*
½ *oz. butter*
2 *egg-whites*
½ *oz. gelatine*
Salt and cayenne pepper

Boil the heads and tails for ten minutes. Scrape flesh away from skin and bone and then pound until it is a smooth creamy paste. Add butter, cream, sherry, cheese and seasoning. Fold in the gelatine powder and mix thoroughly. Cook for fifteen minutes. Set in a cold place for two hours, and then add the egg-whites well beaten. Place in a greased mould, and leave in the refrigerator overnight.

An even cheaper alternative is to use a tin of Canadian salmon, and evaporated milk, well beaten, in place of the butter and cream.

LEG OF LAMB DUXELLES

Small leg of lamb
Garlic, butter and a glass of white wine
Grated Parmesan cheese—1 oz.
¼ *lb. mushrooms*
Teaspoon thyme and parsley stuffing
2 *finely chopped shallots*
1 *oz. breadcrumbs*

Rub the leg well with butter, stick with a few slivers of garlic or a powdering of garlic salt, place in a roasting-tin into which the white wine has been poured. Put into a moderate oven (Regulo 4) and cook for twenty minutes to the pound. Baste frequently (here you would have cause to bless the spit roaster which makes basting so easy). When cooked, place aside and strain off the juice from the pan, clearing the fat.

Deglaze the pan with a little white wine and meat stock. Salt and pepper and add to the juice.

While the lamb is roasting, prepare the filling. Clean and chop the mushrooms finely. Melt some butter into a pan, add the chopped shallots and then the mushrooms with thyme and parsley.

On a brisk flame cook for five minutes. Remove from flame and add the crumbs and seasoning.

Carve the leg, leaving the slices on the bone. In between each slice spread the filling, having care to retain the shape of the leg. Work your 1 oz. of grated Parmesan into the same amount of softened butter and cover the joint with the mixture. A few minutes before you are ready to serve, place in a hot oven to brown.

RUM GÂTEAU

8 *sponge fingers*
1 *oz. walnuts*
1 *oz. butter*
¾ *oz. sugar*
1 *egg*
1 *oz. preserved cherries*
1 *tablespoon of rum*

Cream together the butter and sugar, add the beaten egg, chopped walnuts, cherries and rum.

Dip the sponge fingers in milk, lay four side by side in a shallow dish, and spread the mixture on them. Then lay the remaining four crosswise. Keep in a cold place until ready to serve and then cover with whipped cream and small slices of angelica as decoration.

Canary or other foreign tomatoes are available at a reasonable price. Cod is normally cheap and good in Britain.

Try this dinner.

No. 5 VIENNA TOMATOES
COD À LA GUINGAMPOISE
ANGELS ON HORSEBACK

VIENNA TOMATOES

Take four tomatoes, ¼ lb. sausage meat, salt, pepper, parsley stalks and sprigs.

Cut each tomato in half, season with salt and pepper. Shape the sausage meat into flat cakes, using a little flour to keep the meat together, one for each tomato.

Grill the cakes, and then the tomatoes, taking care to keep the skins intact. Lay the meat cake between the two halves, and decorate with parsley.

COD À LA GUINGAMPOISE

2 cod fillets, ¼ lb. each
Vinegar, pepper, parsley, shallots finely chopped
A clove of garlic, an onion, sliced, and 2 cloves

Cook your fillets lightly and place them aside to cool and dry.

To a quarter-pint water add two dessertspoons of vinegar, a dash of pepper, two sprigs of parsley, two shallots, the garlic, the onion and the cloves. Place the fillets in a shallow dish and add the liquid and the ingredients. Leave to soak for two hours, and then remove, dry and clean off the remains of the ingredients. Coat the fillets with a batter to which a small quantity of grated Gruyère cheese has been added. Roll the coated fillets into the shape of a round of beef. Beat a white of egg lightly and coat the fillets. Fry in hot oil until a golden brown and serve with melted butter or a *hollandaise* sauce. (See Sauces.)

ANGELS ON HORSEBACK

4 chicken livers
4 slices streaky bacon
Toast

Fry the chicken livers and the bacon separately. Wrap the bacon round the livers which have been seasoned with pepper and chopped parsley. Serve on hot toast fingers.

The end of March is approaching. Quarter Day is upon you with the usual influx of bills. To sustain your morale have a really good but simple dinner. It is just about now that Scotch Salmon is at its best, and to my mind there is great pleasure in eating it, plain boiled and hot, with a *mousseline* sauce, and fresh cucumber. Hot-house cucumbers are available, at a price!

No. 6 COLD CONSOMMÉ
BOILED SALMON
POTATO BEIGNETS

COLD CONSOMMÉ

Some excellent cold *consommés* are now available in tins. Alternatively put a good marrow bone through the pressure cooker for about three hours. Leave to cool and skin off the fat. Why buy dripping? The stock will be gelatinous and of good quality. Melt and flavour to taste with beef essence, salt and pepper. Serve cold in jelly form with lemon slices.

BOILED SALMON

I prefer a cut from near the tail of the fish. This is probably pure fancy; any other cut will do. Boil for ten or fifteen minutes according to size. Dry and serve in a clean cloth.

The cucumber will have already been sliced and served with a dash of vinegar and cayenne pepper. The *mousseline* sauce can be prepared while the fish is cooking, though allow for a little extra time in case it goes wrong. (See Sauces.)

POTATO BEIGNETS

Make a good *purée* from four medium-sized floury potatoes. Flavour the *purée* with caster sugar (about a tablespoonful) and either grated orange or lemon peel.

When rolling out the *purée* on a board add a little flour to prevent it sticking. Cut the paste out in circles of about 1¼ inches in diameter. A claret-glass is the right size. Bring a pan of oil to a high temperature and drop your *beignets* in, cooking them until they swell and turn brown. Dust with icing sugar and serve very hot.

No. 1 Crab cocktail
Roast quail
Fresh asparagus

This is an expensive meal, but one with which to welcome the spring. All the items can be bought fresh, but the quail and the asparagus will come from abroad.

CRAB COCKTAIL

This is very similar to a prawn cocktail which has already been described. On a bed of chopped lettuce place your cooked and shredded crab (one large or two small crabs for two people) and add the tomato sauce. Dust with paprika.

ROAST QUAIL

Quails are at their best when freshly killed. Today it is difficult to find them in this condition. Nevertheless, even frozen quail make good eating.

2 quail, plucked and cleaned
4 slices bacon
4 bay leaves

Wrap the quail, first in the bay leaves and then with the bacon. Grill them for ten minutes, turning over from time to time. Serve on fried bread with a slice of lemon, after pouring over them the gravy from the grill pan.

FRESH ASPARAGUS

At this season it is the white asparagus from the Continent that is available. The lower part of the stem is invariably hard and unpalatable and should be cut off. Bundle the upper part, and cook in boiling salted water. After putting in the bundle the water will go off the boil for some minutes. When it comes again to the boil allow fifteen minutes further cooking. Serve with melted butter, *hollandaise* or *vinaigrette* sauce. (See Sauces.)

No. 2 Turtle soup
Lamb cutlets
Cheese tart

TURTLE SOUP

Lusty's turtle soup, either in tins or in solid form, is an excellent starter to a meal. Serve very hot, with a dash of sherry or a quarter of lemon.

LAMB CUTLETS

For two people, four good cutlets
New potatoes, frozen peas

These cutlets can be cooked in a number of ways—plain grilled, or cut from the bone and rolled with half a kidney and a slice of bacon, or boned and larded with slices of orange. On the whole I prefer them salted, peppered and dusted with mixed herbs and then grilled over a hot grill three minutes each side. Don't forget the mint for the potatoes and peas.

CHEESE TART

Line a pastry dish with short pastry. In a bowl mix grated Gruyère cheese, butter, two eggs, a dash of nutmeg, cayenne and salt. Pour the mixture into the dish and cook in a hot oven (Regulo 6).

If you are feeling economical, here are some cheaper dishes.

No. 3 Peach cocktail
Petits pois de cérons
Millas des landes

South African peaches are excellent at this time of year.

PEACH COCKTAIL

Peel and slice one peach per person, place in a fruit glass, add a dash of kirsch and powder with finely chopped almonds.

PETITS POIS DE CÉRONS

Green peas are obtainable all the year round, as is pork.

½ *lb. lean pork*
10 *small onions*
2 *oz. butter*
Large packet frozen peas
Tablespoon of flour
A small lettuce
Herbs

First thaw out your peas. Don't leave them in the refrigerator until the last moment. Then chop the pork up into small dice. Fry gently in butter and add the onions: as soon as these are turning brown, add the flour. Place the peas in a saucepan and mix them with the pork and onions. Chop your lettuce and add it to the mixture with the herbs, the latter preferably in a small muslin bag—the *bouquet garni* in fact. Add a tumbler of water, cover and cook for fifteen minutes until the peas are well done. Season as required, adding a little sugar with the salt.

MILLAS DES LANDES

¼ *lb. maize flour (if obtainable)*
½ *pint hot milk*
¼ *lb. sugar*
3 *eggs*
Grated lemon peel

Mix the hot milk with the flour, add the sugar, the grated lemon peel and stir until the mixture thickens. Then add one by one the yolks of the eggs. Finally, whip the whites and fold into the mixture. Place the mixture in a well-greased cake-tin and cook in a hot oven until nicely browned.

April

MINESTRONE

2 *medium-sized onions*
2 *fresh tomatoes*
1 *carrot*
2 *leeks*
2 *small potatoes*
½ *cabbage*
Parsley, garlic, Parmesan cheese
½ *cup rice*

Brown the onions in butter. Add the tomatoes. Chop the carrot finely with the leeks, the potatoes and the cabbage. Mix together and add half a pint of stock. Bring to boil, add the rice and boil for fifteen minutes. Meanwhile make a paste of chopped garlic, parsley, butter and Parmesan. As soon as the rice is cooked add the paste and stir well.

COD AND TOMATOES

4 *small cod fillets*
½ *lb. fresh tomatoes*
1 *green pimento*
Parsley, a dash of garlic and grated cheese

Poach the cod fillets, remove and dry them carefully.

Meanwhile peel the tomatoes, removing the seeds and the hard stem. Chop the pepper finely with the parsley and dust lightly with garlic salt. In hot oil brown the fillets on both sides and then place, in layers, cod, tomato and the chopped herbs in an open fire-proof dish. Simmer for ten minutes in a slow oven—Regulo 3. Then cover with the grated cheese and brown under the grill.

PASTIS LANDAIS

¼ *lb. flour*
2 *cups of milk*
1 *egg*
¼ *lb. butter*
15 *prunes, stoned*
Sugar, orange water, brandy

Place the flour in a bowl, add 1 cup cold milk, the egg, and a pinch of salt. Mix well and leave to stand for two hours. If the prunes are dry, leave them to soak for the same time.

Then roll out the paste, and scatter over it small lumps of butter. Fold the paste over three times, dusting with flour to prevent sticking. Leave for half an hour. Then cut the paste into two parts and roll out flat. Place the first piece in a well-buttered pie dish and on it lay a layer of the prunes interlarded with dabs of butter. Cover with the second piece of paste, dust with sugar and sprinkle with the orange water and the brandy (personally I would leave out the orange water).

Cook in a moderate oven for ten minutes (Regulo 5).

No. 5 Soupe de la mère Onésime
Fried fillets of plaice
Gâteau au chocolat de Nancy

MÈRE ONÉSIME'S SOUP

This is a typical French peasant's soup that stands reheating and will keep for several days.

¼ *lb. carrots*
¼ *lb. turnip*
2 *oz. of the centre part of a leek*
½ *small cabbage*
Teacup of white beans
Teacup of green peas
Teacup of sliced green beans
¾ *pint good stock*
1 *small sausage—raw*
Tablespoon dripping—heaped
A bouquet garni and a pinch of sugar

Chop the vegetables finely and simmer them in the fat in a covered saucepan, until they soften. Then add half the stock, which should preferably have been made from beef bones or from chicken carcasses. Bring to the boil and skim. Add the *bouquet garni*, and the sugar. Then simmer very gently for three-quarters

94

of an hour. Add the rest of the stock, bring to the boil and add the beans, peas and the sausage. Cook slowly for at least three-quarters of an hour. When serving, remove the *bouquet garni* and clear off any grease. Cut the sausage in small pieces and serve with the soup.

FILLETS OF PLAICE

This is a simple matter of frying the fresh fillets, two per person and serving with a sauce, either anchovy, caper, or *piquante*. Lemon sections will do just as well.

GÂTEAU AU CHOCOLAT DE NANCY

2 oz. butter
2 oz. plain chocolate
2 eggs
2 oz. sugar
Tablespoon flour
Grated almonds and a dash of vanilla flavouring

Work your melted chocolate up with the butter, and add the egg-yolks. Keep stirring. When well mixed add the sugar and the flour. Mix thoroughly and then add the almonds and vanilla. To the mixture add the whites of the eggs well beaten and then place in a well-greased mould. Cook slowly in a moderate oven. The *gâteau* is cooked when it does not stick to a knife passed between it and the tin.

Lobster is very expensive these days and as a main dish almost prohibitive in cost. But a small lobster can be turned into a very appetizing *hors-d'ouvre*.

No. 6 LOBSTER HORS-D'ŒUVRE
CHICKEN PILAF
RASIMAT

LOBSTER HORS-D'ŒUVRE

1 small lobster
2 tablespoons cream

1 *tablespoon brandy*
Grated Parmesan and herbs

Cook the lobster and empty the flesh into a bowl. Keep the shells.

Pound the flesh with the cream, the herbs and the brandy into a smooth mixture. Season with salt and pepper. Put the mixture back into the shells, powder with Parmesan and put under the grill for three minutes.

CHICKEN PILAF

This can be made either with chicken livers, or with the remains of the flesh from a chicken carcass.

Packet chicken livers or ¼ lb. chicken meat
1 oz. chopped almonds
¼ oz. chopped pistachios
¼ lb. mushrooms
3 oz. butter
¼ pint chicken stock
Breakfastcup rice, herbs and bay leaves

Boil the rice for fifteen minutes in the chicken stock with salt and two bay leaves.

Fry the almonds, pistachios and mushrooms together while the rice is cooking. Add a dash of parsley and thyme or origanum if you have it. Add the chicken at the last moment, as the livers cook very quickly and are inclined to disintegrate if over-cooked; and the already cooked chicken bits only need heating. Dry the rice and stir the mixture thoroughly into it.

RASIMAT

Wash and soak ½ lb. of stoned raisins, boil them until quite soft and then pass through a fine sieve. Flavour the *purée* with a dash of brandy, a little sugar to taste, grated lemon rind, and some chopped walnuts. Cook on in same pan until the mixture is sufficiently firm.

No. 1 Moules marinières
Canard aux navets
Zabaglione

Many people like mussels. I don't, but here is a good recipe for this dish. Be it understood straight away that the preparation is laborious even if the beards are not removed. It is essential to clean the mussels most thoroughly, to remove all fibre and sand. Watch out for a particularly heavy one. It may be nothing but a shell where the mussel has died and its place has been taken by sand or clay. One of these that escapes inspection can ruin the whole dish.

2 pints of mussels
2 oz. shallots
Sprig parsley
1 stick celery
1 glass white wine
2 oz. butter

Having washed the mussels, chop the shallots, parsley and celery finely and cook gently in the melted butter. When about half done add the mussels in their shells, and continue cooking for three or four minutes. See that the mussels are covered with the mixture. Then add the white wine and continue cooking for ten minutes. Remove the mussels and take off their top shells. Arrange them on a dish. To the sauce add some crumbled bread to thicken it slightly, some chopped parsley and salt and pepper to taste. Pour the sauce over the mussels and serve.

CANARD AUX NAVETS

This is a good spring dish when the turnips are young and the ducks tender, and not too fat.

1 *small duck*
3 *oz. fat bacon*
Tablespoon flour
1 *pint good stock*
Bouquet garni
Salt and pepper
½ *lb. turnips*
3 *oz. butter*
Dash of sugar and pepper

Allow the best part of two hours for preparation and cooking. In a saucepan just big enough to take the duck, cook the bacon very slowly. Put the duck on top of the bacon, and leaving off the lid, keep the duck turning in the melted bacon fat until it browns. Remove to a dish.

In the saucepan place the flour, and stir until it turns into a brown *roux*. Add the stock, pepper and salt if necessary. Bring to the boil, stirring the whole time. Reduce flame to the simmering level for ten minutes and remove any grease that comes to the surface. Pass the sauce through a sieve into a bowl. Rinse out the saucepan with hot water, and replace the sauce which should now be free from debris. Bring back to the boil and replace the duck and any gravy that it may have made, while waiting. Add the *bouquet garni*. Put the lid on the saucepan and place it in a slow oven for twenty-five minutes. While the duck is cooking, clean and chop the turnips into small cubes. At the end of twenty-five minutes put these cubes into the sauce with the duck and continue the cooking for three-quarters of an hour. Serve the duck with the turnips as garnish, taking care to remove as much of the fat as possible.

ZABAGLIONE

3 *yolks of egg*
1 *tablespoon sugar*
2 *tablespoons sherry*
1 *white of egg*
1 *spoonful lemon juice*

In the upper part of a double saucepan and with a wooden spoon, stir the yolks of egg and the sugar with a lively motion until the mixture begins to cling to the spoon. Then add very slowly the sherry. Place the saucepan in the lower part which should contain sufficient boiling water to cover the lower half of the upper saucepan. Beat the white of egg separately and add it to the mixture, which must be kept stirred and beaten until it turns into a light froth. At the moment of serving add the lemon juice, still beating the mixture. Make sure that it is hot, and serve in warmed fruit glasses.

No. 2 GULLS' EGGS
LAMB CUTLETS GRAMMONT
FONDS D'ARTICHAUT MORNAY

GULLS' EGGS

These are available at this season and can be bought cooked. Serve with brown bread and butter, salt and cayenne pepper.

LAMB CUTLETS GRAMMONT

4 nice lamb cutlets
½ pint béchamel sauce
2 oz. grated Parmesan cheese
2 medium-sized onions
1 egg yolk
Salt, cayenne, parsley and garlic

Slice the onions finely and boil them until soft—about ten minutes. Then rub them through a fine sieve to make a *purée*. Mix this with the *cold béchamel* in a saucepan, adding garlic salt, the egg-yolk, chopped parsley and 1 oz. Parmesan. Grill the cutlets two minutes each side. Line the bottom of a really hot fireproof dish with some of the sauce, and on it rest the cutlets. Add the rest of the sauce and powder with breadcrumbs, chopped parsley and the rest of the Parmesan. Cover the dish with foil or greaseproof paper and heat in the oven at Regulo 9 for seven or eight minutes. This recipe works equally well with veal cutlets.

FONDS D'ARTICHAUT MORNAY

Tins of artichoke hearts are on sale almost everywhere. Fry the artichokes lightly in butter and cover with a *Mornay* sauce (page 60).

No. 3 SMOKED SALMON
PORK CHOPS AUX POMMES EN L'AIR
BRAISED LETTUCE

SMOKED SALMON

Serve with brown bread and butter and lemon quarters.

PORK CHOPS

2 pork chops
3 oz. butter
Potatoes, salt and pepper

Heat the butter in a pan and in it cook the chops one minute each side. Salt and pepper them and lower the heat. Allow to simmer for twenty minutes. Peel and slice the potatoes into fairly thin (¼-inch) slices. Place the chops in a fire-proof dish with their gravy, and surround them with the sliced potatoes. Add salt and pepper, cover the dish with foil and allow to cook in the oven at Regulo 5 until the potatoes are done.

BRAISED LETTUCE

Two well-grown cos lettuces
Butter, salt, pepper, nutmeg

Soak the lettuce in cold water for an hour. Dry and tie firmly with string into bundles. Blanch in boiling salt water for ten minutes. Melt 2 oz. butter in a heavy frying-pan and in it place the lettuce seasoned with salt, pepper and nutmeg.

Simmer gently for half an hour, with the saucepan lid in place. Then add a tablespoon of lemon juice and serve.

No. 4 Bortsch soup
Poulet à l'estragon
Choux à la crème

BORTSCH

There are a number of recipes for bortsch but a fairly simple one that I have used with success requires the following ingredients:

1 *small cabbage*
3 *raw beet*
2 *large onions*
3 *oz. carrots*
½ *lb. tomatoes*
1 *green pepper*
Bouquet garni
Dash of garlic salt, salt, pepper

Chop the vegetables up finely, and allow to simmer for at least two hours in a large covered saucepan. Avoid rapid boiling once the mixture is well heated, as much of the flavour will be lost if this happens. The green pepper does not usually appear in well-known recipes but I add it to cut the sweetness of the beet.

Taste to check the flavour and if satisfactory rub through a coarse sieve. Add the necessary seasoning and serve with cream and beet juice, either hot or cold. Small pastries filled with forcemeat can also be used as garnishing.

POULET À L'ESTRAGON

1 *small roasting chicken*
2 *rashers fat bacon*
Tarragon

Lard the chicken with the bacon and stuff it with the tarragon. Spit roast it, if possible, otherwise roast in the oven in the normal way, twenty minutes per pound weight.

CHOUX À LA CRÈME

To make the *choux* you will need

4 oz. butter
6 oz. flour
Teaspoon salt
Tablespoon caster sugar
4 small eggs
½ pint cold water
Grated lemon peel

Pour the water into a saucepan, add the butter in small morsels, the salt, and the sugar.

Bring to boil slowly so that the butter melts smoothly. Do not put the lid on the saucepan.

As soon as the liquid begins to rise take the saucepan off the flame and pour in all the flour in one go. With a wooden spoon stir the mixture vigorously until it is quite smooth. Replace the saucepan on the flame and allow the paste to dry out, stirring all the time. Take it slowly, otherwise there may be trouble if the heat is too great. The process is more successful if the paste is spread out flat on the bottom of the saucepan and turned over frequently. As soon as the paste comes away cleanly from the pan it is done.

Now is the time to add the eggs, one by one, to the paste, continuing to stir each one until it is well incorporated. It is perhaps wise to beat the eggs lightly before adding them to the pan. Finally, mix in the grated lemon peel.

The final mixture should be stiff enough to keep its shape when squeezed out on to the board in whatever form you prefer, leaving space for the cream lining. Coat lightly with whisked egg. Cook in an open pan for twenty-five minutes in a slow oven (Regulo 4).

When the pastries are a golden colour, and firm to the touch, remove from the oven and leave to cool. Then insert the cream lining with a small funnel and the *choux* are ready. The cream can be given a variety of flavours. Probably sugar and a dash of orange juice is best.

I do not, as I have said, like Chinese food, but as a change, the following recipes are worth considering. The special ingredients have to be bought in tins, but most delicatessen shops sell them.

FRIED NOODLES WITH BEAN SPROUTS AND PORK

½ *lb. egg noodles*
2 *oz. bean sprouts*
Tablespoon soy sauce.
¼ *lb. lean pork*

Chop the bean sprouts and pork finely. Boil the noodles for five minutes, rinse and drain. Then put them in a deep fry for five minutes until they are crisp and brown. Place in dish and keep hot. Fry the chopped bean sprouts and pork for three minutes, mix with the soy sauce and place on top of the noodles.

LITCHI DELIGHT

5 *oz. Amoy litchis*
1 *oz. marshmallows*
⅛ *th pint cream*
Dessertspoon caster sugar
Chopped nuts
Small sponge cake

Drain the litchis and chop them finely. Cut the marshmallows into small pieces and mix with the litchis. Keep cool for three hours.

Then whip the cream, add the sugar and fold into the fruit mixture. Cover the sponge cake with the mixture and decorate with the nuts.

No. 6 FISH SOUP
VEAL CHOPS WITH GRAPEFRUIT
WILD STRAWBERRIES

FISH SOUP

½ *lb. sorrel*
1 *lettuce heart*
2 *ozs. leek*
2 *oz. butter*
1 *egg, chervil*
Fish stock

Chop the vegetables and let them simmer in 1 oz. butter for twenty minutes. Then add half a pint of the fish stock and a tablespoon of chervil from which the stalks have been removed. Simmer again for fifteen minutes and then add the rest of the stock. Remove the saucepan from the flame and mix in the egg. Add 1 oz. butter in small lumps and when melted and mixed the soup can be served on thick slices of bread in the soup dish.

VEAL CHOPS WITH GRAPEFRUIT

2 *veal chops*
3 *oz. butter*
2 *grapefruit*
1 *liqueur glass brandy*
1 *glass dry white wine*
2 *carrots, pinch of thyme, bay leaf*

Scrape and clean the carrots, and cut them into fine slices. In a fire-proof dish melt the butter and add the carrots and chops. Cook gently, turning the chops over so that they brown on both sides. When nicely brown, add salt, pepper and the brandy well alight. When *flambé* add the white wine and then the thyme, the bay leaf and the juice of one grapefruit. Cook very slowly for ten minutes and then dish up, decorating the chops with slices of the second grapefruit, without the skin.

A good accompaniment is noodles fried in butter.

WILD STRAWBERRIES WITH KIRSCHWASSER

The French wild strawberry, known as the *quatre saisons*, is available towards the end of May. Serve with plenty of sugar, whipped cream and a tablespoon of Kirschwasser.

JUNE MENUS

No. 1 Eggs with mushroom stuffing
Pork chops marinées
Ginger log

EGGS WITH MUSHROOMS

2 *eggs*
3 *oz. mushrooms*
1 *oz. butter*
S*alt, pepper, mixed herbs or chopped tarragon*
Béchamel sauce and grated cheese

Hard-boil the eggs; remove the yolks into a bowl. Cook the chopped mushrooms lightly in butter. Grease a small fire-proof dish and cover the bottom with two-thirds of the cooked and chopped mushrooms.

Add one-third chopped mushrooms and herbs to the yolks, mix well with salt and pepper. Then stuff the eggs with this mixture. Place the eggs on the bed of mushrooms and over them pour the *béchamel* which has been flavoured with the grated cheese. Dust lightly with grated Parmesan and put under the grill for five minutes.

PORK CHOPS MARINÉES

2 *pork chops*
½ *pint vegetable oil*
2 *bay leaves*
2 *cloves*
Salt and pepper

Place the chops in an open dish. Cover with the oil, bay leaves, cloves, salt and pepper. Leave for three days in a cool place, turning the chops over night and morning.

Pour in sufficient of the marinade to cover the bottom of a pan and heat the chops in it until they are a golden brown; leave to cook gently. When ready to serve, place in a serving dish and cover with a hot *Sauce Robert.* (See Sauces page 62.)

GINGER LOG

¼ lb. ginger crisps
½ pint cream
Chopped walnuts
Chocolate sauce
Sugar and rum to taste

Whip the cream lightly and add the rum and sugar. Put this mixture in between the crisps so as to form a 'log'. Wrap in greaseproof paper and leave in refrigerator for twenty-four hours. When about to serve, cover with chocolate sauce and fleck with whipped cream. Serve with hot chocolate sauce flavoured with rum and chopped walnuts. Cut diagonally when serving.

No. 2 PEA SOUP
RATATOUILLE
BRANDY PEACHES

PEA SOUP

Green peas are now available. If you have served the peas as a vegetable, you will have kept the pods for soup.

The pods from 1 lb. peas
2 shallots
Salt and pepper

Boil the pods until they are well softened. Keep the stock. Rub the pods through a sieve to make a *purée.* Then slice the shallots finely, place them with the *purée*, salt and pepper and sufficient of the stock and simmer gently for an hour. Strain and serve.

RATATOUILLE

Aubergines and small marrows are now available.

2 medium-sized aubergines
3 tomatoes

June

1 *green pepper*
1 *small marrow*
Salt, pepper, dash of garlic

Peel, slice and salt the aubergines and marrow, removing seeds and pips. Skin the tomatoes and take out the hard centre and pips. Slice the pepper, removing the seeds carefully. Place the vegetables in hot oil and cook until soft. Add garlic, salt, and pepper and simmer for an hour, stirring occasionally. Remove to a fireproof dish, cover with grated Parmesan cheese and place under the grill for five minutes. The expert's recipe for ratatouille is much as above, but it is allowed to simmer for three days! Few people have the patience or the facilities. Another form calls for sliced onions for which I have a preference.

BRANDY PEACHES

2 *large peaches*
2 *tablespoons brandy*
2 *oz. caster sugar*
Whipped cream and blanched almonds

Mix the brandy and sugar thoroughly. Dip the peaches in boiling water for an instant (they must not soften) and then in cold water. Dry them thoroughly, when the peel will come off quite easily. Cut in half and remove the stones. Quarter them, place them in a bowl and pour over them the brandy sauce. Leave to stand for at least two hours. Stir from time to time. Serve with the whipped cream and grated almonds.

No. 3 SOLE À LA RUSSE
CHEESE SOUFFLÉ
STRAWBERRIES AND CREAM

SOLE À LA RUSSE

1 *sole of about ¾ lb.*
3 *fresh carrots, for preference not thicker than ¾ inch, even better less than this*

1 *large onion*
Bunch parsley
4 *oz. butter*
Dessertspoon lemon juice, salt, pepper

Slice the carrots about $\frac{1}{16}$-inch thick and as evenly as possible to help regular cooking. If the slices are too thick they will take too long to cook; if too thin they will break up while cooking. Slice the onion in the same way. Place the vegetables with half the butter in a small saucepan and cook gently for fifteen minutes. See that the vegetables are soft. Add half a pint of water and a pinch of salt and bring to the boil. Lower the flame until just simmering and add the rest of the butter. Allow to cook very gently for another twenty minutes. Five minutes before the end of the cooking add the finely chopped parsley. Having trimmed the sole place it in a fire-proof dish that has been well greased. Over it pour the vegetables with their liquid. Bring to the boil and then allow to simmer gently. Cover the dish with foil and allow to simmer for another twenty minutes, basting the fish from time to time with the liquid. Before serving add a little butter in pats to further moisten the dish, and then sprinkle with the lemon juice.

CHEESE SOUFFLÉ

Most *soufflés* can now be bought in packets and are very little trouble to make. But a home-made *soufflé* is better. It requires:

2 *oz. butter*
Breakfastcup grated cheese (Canadian cheddar)
2 *level tablespoons self-raising flour*
2 *eggs*
Salt, pepper, breakfastcup milk

Grease the *soufflé* dish and in it cream the butter, flour, salt and pepper over the flame. Add the milk and when well mixed, remove from the heat.

Separate the whites of the eggs from the yolks and quickly beat in the yolks one at a time. Add the grated cheese. Then beat the whites until they are really stiff. Fold the whip in with the other ingredients and cook in a hot oven (Regulo 5) for twenty-five minutes.

By this time the housewife will have had enough of cooking and the strawberries will come as a relief.

No. 4 SOLE AU VIN BLANC (Roman style)
STUFFED BOILED CABBAGE
FRIED DATES WITH HONEY

SOLE AU VIN BLANC (APICIUS)

Try Apicius' version of *sole au vin blanc,* as described in his cookery book mentioned on page 12, Chapter I.

A fine sole of ¾ lb.
Oil, wine, pepper, origanum fish stock
1 egg

Clean the sole and place in a shallow dish; add oil and wine. In a saucepan put half a pint of fish stock with the pepper and origanum and work in the raw egg to make a smooth mixture. Pour over the sole and cook over a low fire for twenty minutes.

Although Apicius does not specify the colour of the wine, try a dry white or dry vermouth.

Now we pass from ancient Rome to modern Scandinavia.

STUFFED BOILED CABBAGE

1 large white cabbage
½ lb. forcemeat
1 egg.
Flour, cold boiled milk, salt, pepper

The forcemeat can be made from minced veal, or pork and veal mixed, and a little flour, seasoning, a raw egg and enough milk to moisten the mixture. Slice a 'lid' from the stalk end of the cabbage and cut out the hard stem so as to make a hollow large enough to hold the forcemeat. Stuff the cabbage, tie on the 'lid' carefully and wrap the whole in muslin. Simmer very slowly for three hours and then drain. When serving cut it like a cake and add melted butter.

FRIED DATES WITH HONEY

½ *lb. best dates*
2 *oz. blanched almonds*
2 *tablespoons honey*

Now we are back in Rome. Stone the dates and stuff with almonds. Roll in salt and fry in the honey. The recipe also calls for pine kernels, but I suggest omitting these!

No. 5 Fish soup
Canard aux herbes
Danish cherry tart

FISH SOUP

½ *lb. fresh haddock*
1 *small onion*
1 *carrot*
1 *tomato*
¾ *oz. butter*
1 *oz. flour*
1 *pint milk*
Dash turmeric, garlic salt, pepper, salt

Chop the onion and carrot finely and fry in butter—do not brown. Add the fish chopped small. Peel and empty the tomato of seed and hard stem, and join it to the fish, carrot and onion, together with the flour. Stir in the milk and cook slowly. Powder with garlic salt, salt and pepper. Lastly add enough turmeric to turn the soup a pale yellow. If the soup thickens too much, add more milk until it turns into a thin *purée*.

CANARD AUX HERBES

A small duck
4 *oz. butter*
2 *large onions*
Glass of white wine

½ *lemon*
Dessertspoon flour
Sprig parsley, thyme, bay, basil, a clove
Salt and pepper

Cook the duck lightly in 2 oz. butter. Pepper and salt it and put the herbs (in a *bouquet garni*) with it into a casserole. Add the wine and cover the casserole. Cook slowly in a medium oven (Regulo 5) according to its size. Chop the onion finely and brown with the rest of the butter. Add the flour and pour into this mixture the gravy from the casserole. Reduce this sauce to the consistency of a thin *purée*. Add the juice from the half lemon.

When the duck is cooked (test it for tenderness with a fork) carve it and place on the serving dish. Cover it with the onion sauce and serve.

DANISH CHERRY TART

Short pastry
½ *lb. stoned cooking cherries (Morello)*
4 *oz. ground almonds*
6 *oz. sieved icing sugar*
2 *eggs*
⅓ *pint cream*

Line a flan tin with the pastry. Prick the pastry well. Fill the tin with the cherries. Mix the ground almonds with the icing sugar. Add the eggs, one at a time, until the mixture has the consistency of soft paste. Pour this over the cherries and bake at Regulo 7 for twenty-five to thirty minutes. Serve cold with whipped cream.

No. 6 AVOCADO PEARS
SWISS FONDUE
FROSTED ORANGES

AVOCADO PEARS

2 *pears*
Small packet peeled shrimps
Hollandaise sauce. (See page 56.)

Cut the pears in half, remove the stones and fill with the shrimps. Keep cool and serve with *hollandaise* sauce.

SWISS FONDUE

It is possible to buy the *fondue* in tins. Here is the recipe. Rub an earthenware dish round with a cut clove of garlic. Pour in two wineglasses of a dry white wine. Salt and pepper. Bring to the boil. Add ½ lb. of finely grated Gruyère cheese, and stir until it is melted into the boiling wine. Finish with a tablespoon of kirsch. Serve over a heater so that the mixture is always on the boil.

Prepare toast strips which are dipped into the *fondue* and eaten in the fingers.

FROSTED ORANGES

4 oranges
½ lb. sugar

Cut the caps off the oranges, remove the pulp, without injuring the skins, squeeze and set the juice aside.
Put the sugar in a saucepan with ½ pint water and heat to 86° on a sugar thermometer. Remove from the flame, add the orange juice and heat to 66°.

Leave to cool and before it sets fill the orange skins with the liquid. Freeze, and before serving dust with caster sugar.

JULY MENUS

No. 1 Sorrel soup
Braised ham
Kuller pfirsich

SORREL SOUP

½ *lb. chopped sorrel*
4 *oz. butter*
3 *oz. flour*
2 *eggs*
¼ *pint milk*

Cook the sorrel very slowly in 3 oz. butter for about twenty minutes. Add the flour and keep on stirring over a low flame until the flour takes on a light yellow colour. Then pour on a pint of boiling water, with salt and a pinch of sugar. Put the lid on the saucepan and allow to simmer for another twenty minutes.

Beat up the eggs with the milk and add to the soup, by now off the boil. When ready to serve remove from the flame, and add the remaining ounce of butter.

BRAISED HAM

4 *slices of ham*
2 *wineglasses madeira*
Spoonful brown sugar
4 *cloves*

Place the ham in an open dish, cover with the madeira, add the sugar and cloves.

Cover with foil and cook gently for twenty minutes at Regulo 3. The sugar should be completely melted and the wine reduced to about half the quantity. Serve with spinach and new potatoes.

KULLER PFIRSICH (Rolling peaches)

2 *large fresh peaches in their skins.* (Another recipe advises peeling the peaches.)
¼ *bottle champagne*
Tablespoon caster sugar

H 113

Prick the peaches all over with a fork. Powder with the sugar and put to soak in the champagne for an hour. Serve in an open glass dish. The champagne can accompany the fruit.

Some people find this dish very intoxicating so care must be taken as to the quantity of liquor consumed beforehand.

No. 2 YOGHOURT SOUP

POULET SAUTÉ À LA PORTUGAISE

CRÈME ST. HONORÉ

YOGHOURT SOUP

2 cartons yoghourt
Worcester sauce

Mix the yoghourt with the Worcester sauce to taste and add salt if thought necessary.

POULET SAUTÉ

1 small chicken
2 oz. butter
2 tablespoons vegetable oil
¼ lb. mushrooms
2 medium-sized onions chopped fine
3 large ripe tomatoes
1 tumbler of stock
1 tumbler white wine
Dessertspoon tomato purée
Dash garlic salt, chopped parsley, salt, pepper

Cut up the chicken into the wings, breast and legs.

Heat the oil to smoking point in a saucepan big enough to take all the bits lying flat, skin side down. As soon as the bits are in the saucepan reduce the flame to a gentle heat. Cook uncovered and without touching the meat for five minutes. Then lift to see if the underside is nicely brown. If so, turn over to let the tops cook.

As soon as the wings and breast are cooked take them out and place on a dish. Keep warm. Continue cooking the legs for another ten minutes and then place with the rest of the bird.

Meanwhile the sauce has to be prepared.

Chop the mushrooms into thick slices. Peel and empty the tomatoes of seeds and core. Add a little more oil to the remains in the saucepan and cook the mushrooms in it. Let them dry out in a sieve.

Take all the oil out of the saucepan and cook the onions in 2 oz. butter. Do not allow them to colour. Add the tomatoes and cook for five minutes. Add the white wine, and allow to boil vigorously until almost complete reduction of the liquid. Then put in the mushrooms, the garlic salt, the stock, the tomato *purée*, salt and pepper. Put the lid on the saucepan and allow to simmer for ten minutes.

Then place the meat in the saucepan and cover it well with the sauce. Cover and allow to simmer for another five minutes.

Place the meat on a serving dish. If the sauce is thin, add a small quantity of *béchamel* sauce. When the consistency is right, pour over the chicken and dress with chopped parsley.

CRÈME ST. HONORÉ

A sweet very popular in France and dedicated to the patron saint of pastry cooks.

½ *pint milk*
4 *oz. flour*
4 *oz. sugar*
2 *eggs*
2 *teaspoons gelatine*
A few drops of vanilla flavouring

Beat the yolks with the sugar and flour. Add very slowly to the boiling milk flavoured with the vanilla and in which the gelatine has been dissolved. Bring slowly to the boil and stir continuously. Beat the whites firmly and add them gradually to the mixture. Serve cold.

July

No. 3 STUFFED CELERY

FILET EN CROÛTE

COQUE AU LAIT

STUFFED CELERY

Celery is available towards the end of this month.

1 *stick celery*
1 *oz grated Gruyère cheese*
Tablespoon cream
Cayenne pepper

Choose stems of the celery that are tender and concave. Mix the cheese with the cream and fill the hollow in the celery stem with the mixture. Dust with cayenne and serve very cold.

FILET EN CROÛTE

½ *lb. rolled fillet of beef*
Puff pastry mix
Mixed herbs, pepper and salt

If fillet of beef is difficult to get, good tender rump will do almost as well. Salt, pepper and dust with herbs. Grill over a very hot grill for just long enough to seal the meat. Roll in the puff pastry to make a 'log'. Cook in a hot oven Regulo 7 for twenty-five minutes. Serve with fried mushrooms.

COQUE AU LAIT

½ *pint milk*
3 *eggs*
¼ *lb. granulated sugar*
Tablespoon fresh cream
Liqueur glass of armagnac or brandy

Into an oven mould put the sugar, the cream, 3 yolks and 1 white of egg and mix well for two minutes. Bring the milk to the boil and add very slowly to the mixture, stirring all the time. Then add the armagnac or brandy. In a slow oven (Regulo 4) cook for twenty minutes. When cool, chill the mixture and turn out of the mould. Serve very cold.

July

No. 4 STUFFED AUBERGINES
CANARD AUX ÉCHALOTES
RASPBERRY CREAM

One large aubergine
2 tablespoons oil
2 medium onions
2 tomatoes
Pinch garlic powder
Dessertspoon grated cheese
1 oz. combined butter, salt, pepper, mixed herbs

Cut the aubergine in half and cut the flesh across without damaging the skin. Rub with salt. Leave for twenty minutes, and then place with the inside downwards in the hot oil. Fry for five minutes, turning over once or twice. When brown, lift out and carefully scrape out the flesh, which should then be chopped up.

Chop and cook the onions and tomatoes in butter. Mix with the aubergine flesh and the seasoning and stuff the aubergine skins with the mixture. Powder with the grated cheese and heat under the grill.

CANARD AUX ÉCHALOTES

A small duck
½ lb. beef dripping
4 shallots
Wineglass red wine
Thyme and bay
Coffee-spoon meat extract
4 oz. butter
Salt, pepper

Chop two shallots finely, also half the duck's liver. Grate the dripping and mix with the shallots and liver. Stuff the duck with the mixture. Lard the bird with half the butter and put to roast in the oven at Regulo 6. Do not let it overcook!

Then chop the remaining shallots with the half liver and place in a saucepan with the red wine, sprig of thyme, a bay leaf, salt and pepper. When the liquid is reduced by half, add the meat extract. Reduce further and when ready to serve add the remains of the butter, lump by lump, stirring briskly. Remove the herbs and pour round the duck on the serving plate. On a spit roaster the cooking can be watched very closely and basting is simple. This is important as the duck meat should be pink—almost *saignant*.

RASPBERRY CREAM

¾ lb. fresh raspberries
⅓ pint cream
Teacup of milk
Tablespoon caster sugar
¼ oz. gelatine
Juice of half lemon
Tablespoon raspberry syrup

Boil the raspberries in a small quantity of water and rub them through a sieve. Dissolve the sugar and gelatine in the milk, add the lemon juice and raspberry syrup and mix with the raspberry pulp. Then stir in the stiffly whipped cream, place in a mould, and chill in the lower part of the refrigerator.

No. 5 SMOKED TROUT
BLANQUETTE DE VEAU
SUMMER PUDDING

SMOKED TROUT

Serve with lemon or a *Sauce piquante*. (See page 59.)

BLANQUETTE DE VEAU

¾ lb. neck of veal
1 *large onion*
¼ lb. carrots cut fine
Bouquet garni and a few celery tops
3 *oz. butter*
¼ lb. mushrooms
2 *egg-yolks*
⅓ pint cream
Grated nutmeg, lemon juice, chopped parsley
Salt and pepper

118

The veal is cut into small cubes, about ½-inch in size and heaped in a deep and narrow saucepan so that the meat can be covered without too much *cold* water. Add salt. Bring slowly to the boil, stirring the veal so that the scum comes to the surface; clear with a spoon and add more cold water from time to time. Carry on for thirty minutes by which time all the scum will have come to the surface. Remove it carefully. Then add the carrots, the onion pricked with one or two cloves, and the *bouquet garni*. Bring back to the boil, partly cover the saucepan and allow to simmer for a full hour. Do not let the meat get mushy from over-cooking. Meanwhile, fry the peeled mushrooms (about ¼ lb.) and then a dozen small onions.

With the butter and two heaped tablespoons of flour make a *roux*. This should take about six to eight minutes. Pour the veal stock through a sieve and set aside; put the meat into a bowl. Keep warm. With some of the stock make a sauce with the *roux*. Bring to the boil, add the mushroom peelings, pepper and a little nutmeg. Allow to cook thoroughly then slowly pass through a sieve, and then mix in the egg-yolks, the cream and the lemon juice.

Replace the meat in a saucepan, add the small onions and peeled mushrooms. Re-heat and when hot enough, place on the serving dish and cover with the sauce. Add chopped parsley and serve. Keep the balance of the stock in the refrigerator. It will be needed for the next menu.

SUMMER PUDDING

¾ *lb. red currants*
6 *slices of white bread*
Sugar
⅓ *pint cream*

Boil the red currants in two breakfastcups of water, with sugar added to taste. Strain the fruit and form into a flat-topped pyramid on the serving-plate. Surround the fruit with the slices of bread and cover with the liquid. Alternatively, line a bowl with the bread and heap the fruit in the middle. Chill in the refrigerator and serve cold with cream. Serve extra juice and cream.

No. 6 BORTSCH À LA RUSSE
CHICKEN KIEVSKY
HERRING ROES ON TOAST

BORTSCH À LA RUSSE

This is a slightly simpler version of the bortsch recipe given earlier and is a good way of using up the veal stock referred to in the previous menu.

¼ *lb. carrots*
1 *onion* } *all finely chopped*
3 *small beet*

Place in a saucepan with just enough boiling water to cover them. Cook for twenty minutes on a low flame. Then add

1 *tablespoon butter*
½ *pint veal stock*
2 *oz. cabbage finely shredded*
4 *tomatoes peeled and cleaned*

Boil for fifteen minutes. Serve with sour cream or grated cucumber.

CHICKEN KIEVSKY

2 *boned wings of chicken*
Batter
3 *oz. butter*
Pepper, salt and breadcrumbs

Fry the chicken wings in 2 oz. butter, pepper and salt, until they are golden colour. Work the batter in a thin layer round them, leaving a gap on the top side.

Pepper the batter with breadcrumbs and then fry till brown. Cut a gash in the meat along the gap and when ready to serve melt the remainder of the butter and pour into the gash.

ROES ON TOAST

Toast fingers
4 *herring roes*

Pepper and salt
1 *oz. butter*
Chopped parsley

Fry the roes in butter, place them on the toast fingers, add chopped parsley and serve very hot.

No. 1 Bayonne ham with fresh figs
Cold hake. Mayonnaise sauce
Coffee mousse

HAM AND FIGS

Serve the ham in very thin slices with fresh figs well chilled.

HAKE AND MAYONNAISE SAUCE

4 *Hake steaks—¼ lb. each*
Fish stock with herbs
Mayonnaise sauce. (See pages 55, 56.)

Poach the steaks in a saucepan with enough water to cover them for about ten minutes. Remove the steaks and add 4 bay leaves, thyme, salt, 2 carrots, and 2 small onions chopped up, parsley, tablespoon wine vinegar, pepper to the stock.

Allow to boil for half an hour and then leave to cool. When cold replace the steaks and cook very gently. Lower the heat the moment the stock shows signs of boiling, and then simmer for five minutes. Remove the steaks, skin and bone them and leave to cool.

Serve with the *mayonnaise*.

COFFEE MOUSSE

2 *eggs*
1 *teacup cream*
½ *teacup strong black coffee*
Dessertspoon powdered gelatine
1 *tablespoon caster sugar*

Separate the eggs and beat the yolks thoroughly with the sugar. Beat the whites into a very stiff froth. Do the same with the cream until it clings to the beater. Stir the cold black coffee into the egg-yolks.

Meanwhile the gelatine has been dissolving in a small quantity of water. Melt this mixture over a very low flame and stir into the egg-yolks. Add the sugar and stir until the mixture thickens, and then fold in the beaten whites very carefully. Add the cream and stir it in thoroughly though gently. Keep stirring until the *mousse* starts to stiffen. Pour into a mould and chill.

Serve with cream.

No. 2 POTATO AND LEEK SOUP
EGGS BIGARRADE
PÊCHES FLAMBÉES

POTATO AND LEEK SOUP

½ *lb. leeks*
2 *large potatoes*
2 *carrots*
2 *onions* } *small and chopped*
1 *stick celery, chopped*
1½ *pints chicken stock*
2 *oz. butter*
2 *tablespoons cream*
Parsley chopped, 2 bay leaves, salt, pepper

Braise the chopped vegetables very lightly in 1 oz. butter. Add the leeks and another ounce of butter. As soon as the leeks soften pour on the stock and add the potatoes sliced thin, salt, pepper and the bay leaves. Cover and cook gently for three-quarters of an hour. Add the parsley and continue to cook for five minutes. Remove the bay leaves and rub through a sieve, or, if you have an electric mixer such as the Paladin, make the *purée* in it. Replace the *purée* in the saucepan with the bay leaves and continue to cook very gently for ten minutes. Serve with a dash of cream in each plate.

EGGS BIGARRADE

4 *eggs*
1 *orange*
1 *tablespoon sweet liqueur such as* Grand Marnier *or* Cointreau
1 *teaspoon orange juice*
1 *teaspoon lemon juice*
Salt, *pepper and tomato sauce.*

Peel the orange and blanch the rind in boiling water. Cut into thin strips *à la julienne.* Put aside. Remove the inner rind of the orange and cut in four slices. Place with the *julienne.*

Prepare the tomato sauce from:

6 *tomatoes, peeled, seeded and chopped*
1 *small onion chopped*
¼ *pint stock*
1 *oz. butter*
Bouquet garni
Pepper, flour

Cook the onion in a small frying-pan with the butter; add pepper, salt and the tomatoes; sprinkle with a teaspoon of flour and pour on the stock. Add the *bouquet garni* and simmer until almost completely reduced. Remove the *bouquet garni* and rub the contents of the pan through a sieve. Heat again with a dab of butter.

Over a very low flame pour the liqueur, the orange and lemon juice into the sauce, and mix well. Put aside to keep hot.

Soft boil the eggs and peel them. Place the slices of orange in a hot buttered dish and on top of them put the eggs. Pepper and salt, cover with the *julienne* and pour on the sauce. Serve immediately before the eggs start to hard-boil.

PÊCHES FLAMBÉES

2 *large fresh peaches*
1 *tablespoon caster sugar*
1 *tablespoon brandy*

Peel the peaches. Place them in a warmed dish, cover with the sugar and heat gently. When ready, heat the brandy in a spoon, light it and pour over the peaches.

No. 3 CHAKCHOUKA
CROQUETTES DE VOLAILLE
MARROW ON TOAST

CHAKCHOUKA

Ratatouille
4 *eggs*

Prepare a small ratatouille (see page 106), sufficient to fill the bottom of a shallow Pyrex dish. With a spoon, make four hollows in the mixture, and break an egg into each one. Place the dish in a hot oven (Regulo 8) and serve straight from the dish as soon as the eggs are lightly cooked.

CROQUETTES DE VOLAILLE

½ *lb. cooked chicken and stuffing, chopped fine*
1 *white of egg*
2 *oz. butter*
2 *tablespoons oil*
Flour
4 *oz. potato purée.* (See Potatoes.)

First make the potato *purée* incorporating the egg-yolk and mix it with the chopped chicken and stuffing and a tablespoon of grated cheese. When cool, roll into croquettes and dip into the white of egg. Roll in the flour. Meanwhile heat the oil and butter together in a frying-pan and brown the croquettes in the mixture. Serve at once.

MARROW ON TOAST

2 *square slices of white bread*
Beef marrow
Salt, pepper

Your butcher will empty a good marrow bone for you in one piece. Slice the marrow in ½-inch slices and place on the two pieces of bread. Salt and pepper, place in a shallow fire-proof dish and cook in a hot oven (Regulo 9). As soon as the marrow begins to brown, remove and serve. Some people like the marrow with a few drops of lemon juice on it. I agree.

No. 4 RAW VEGETABLES. SAUCE BAGNAROTTE
LA PIPERADE
BACON AND PRUNES

VEGETABLES AND SAUCE

Cauliflower, celery, carrots, radishes, cole slaw (chopped heart of cabbage) each in small quantities and arranged decoratively in an open dish.

Sauce Bagnarotte consists of:

Breakfastcup mayonnaise. (See pages 55, 56.)
2 dessertspoons tomato ketchup
2 teaspoons fresh cream
2 coffee-spoons Worcestershire sauce
2 coffee-spoons cognac
Dash tabasco, some drops lemon juice, salt and pepper

Mix all these ingredients together and serve cold. The vegetables should be cut so that they can be eaten in the fingers or on cocktail sticks after dipping in the sauce.

LA PIPERADE

This is scrambled eggs *à la Basque*.

4 eggs
4 tomatoes, peeled, seeded and chopped
4 fresh green peppers (boil for ten minutes if not quite fresh)
1 tablespoon oil
1 oz. diced bacon
Dash garlic sauce
1 small onion chopped fine
1 oz. butter, salt, pepper

Heat the butter and oil in a frying-pan. In the pan cook the bacon, the green peppers (previously softened if not fresh) and the onion. Add the garlic and tomatoes, salt and pepper. Increase the heat and crush the tomatoes to get rid of the water in them. Just before the vegetables are cooked (ten to fifteen minutes) add the four eggs, well beaten together. Keep stirring until the eggs are scrambled, and serve.

BACON SAVOURY

4 rashers lean bacon
4 prunes, stoned
4 toast fingers

Wrap the rashers round the prunes, pin with a cocktail stick and cook under the grill. Serve on the toast.

No. 5 COLD HORS-D'ŒUVRE
GRILLED LOBSTER À LA DIABLE
LITCHIS IN SYRUP WITH CREAM

COLD HORS-D'ŒUVRE

Chopped red cabbage with French dressing.
Sliced cucumber—in vinegar
Anchovies
Eggs stuffed with tunny fish

These items are self-explanatory.

GRILLED LOBSTER

Small lobster, about 1½ lb.
2 tablespoons vegetable oil
2 tablespoons fresh cream
2 tablespoons butter
2 tablespoons armagnac or brandy
Herbs, salt, pepper

Split the lobster in half and pull off the claws. Heat the oil in a frying-pan until it begins to smoke and in it plunge the bits of lobster, meat side down. Add the claws. Keep the bits pressed down in the pan for four minutes and then remove. Leave the claws in the oil for another ten minutes.

In a fire-proof dish place bits with the cut side uppermost, and the claws. Spread the cream, butter and herbs on the bits and grill for ten minutes. Baste frequently. Remove the lobster and break the claws. Place in a well-warmed dish. Heat the spirit in a tablespoon, light it and pour over the lobster. Serve immediately.

LITCHIS IN SYRUP

Tinned litchis are available at most delicatessen shops. Serve with whipped cream.

No. 6 FONDS D'ARTICHAUTS
ROGNONS PAMPLONA
MARTINIQUE EGG

FONDS D'ARTICHAUTS

These can be bought tinned or bottled or the heart and base can be taken from fresh boiled artichokes. Serve with French dressing or a *mousseline* sauce. (See page 57.)

ROGNONS PAMPLONA

4 *lambs' kidneys*
1 *breakfastcup Patna-type rice*
2 *tomatoes, peeled, seeded and chopped*
1 *red sweet pepper (tinned)*
2 *oz. mushrooms*
2 *oz. cooked peas*
1 *small onion, chopped*
1 *wineglass sherry*
1 *tablespoon olive oil*
Pat butter
Salt, pepper, chopped parsley, garlic salt

Put the rice on to boil for fifteen minutes in salt water with two bay leaves.

Fry the peeled mushrooms in the butter for five minutes. Keep them separate so they cook evenly. Place aside and keep hot. Cut the kidneys in half, wash thoroughly and remove the outer skin and hard centre. Chop roughly and fry in very hot oil for not more than two minutes. Add the chopped onion and allow to colour. Then add the garlic and the butter. Stir and pour in the sherry. Allow to reduce a little and then add the tomatoes. A minute later add the cooked peas and mushrooms. Mix carefully, using a wooden spoon. Salt and pepper and set aside. By this time the rice will be cooked. Drain, wash, and dry in the oven. When dry place in the serving-dish, make a hollow in the middle, and over it pour the contents of the pan. Cut the sweet peppers *en julienne*, and heat them. Scatter the parsley over the rice and decorate the dish with the strips of red pepper.

Heat once more in the oven and then serve.

MARTINIQUE EGG

1 *slice pineapple*
½ *peach*
Whipped cream
Rum

In a glass dish place the slice of pineapple. On the pineapple put the half peach. Arrange the whipped cream round the peach so that it looks like a fried egg. Add a little good rum and serve very cold.

No. 1 Cold fillets Sole Duglére
Porc à l'orange
Champignon mornay

SOLE FILLETS—SAUCE DUGLÉRÉ

4 *fillets sole*
4 *large tomatoes*
2 *chopped shallots*
Chopped parsley
½ *pint mayonnaise sauce*
Glass white wine

Grease a fish dish, sprinkle with the chopped shallots, parsley, season with salt and pepper and the *tomates concassées*. On these place the fillets of sole, add the glass of white wine and a little fish stock, cover with a greased paper, bring to the boil on the stove, then place in oven to cook for ten minutes.

Take out the fish and place in the serving dish to cool. Place the stock on top of stove to reduce, allow it to cool off, then stir in the *mayonnaise* sauce. Mask the fillets with this sauce, and sprinkle a little chopped parsley.

PORC À L'ORANGE

1 *lb. loin of pork*
1 *veal knuckle bone*
2 *medium carrots, diced*
2 *oz. butter*
2 *oranges*
Wineglass brandy
Wineglass white wine
¼ *pint stock*
Bouquet garni
Arrowroot, salt and pepper

Place the meat in a saucepan and brown it all over in the butter.

130

Add salt and pepper. Heat the brandy and pour it over the meat when it is well alight. When no longer alight add the knuckle bone, the *bouquet* and the carrots. Pour on the white wine and the stock, cover and allow to simmer until the pork is tender (about 1½ hours).

Peel the oranges and blanch the rind in boiling water. Cool and cut into very thin strips. Squeeze one orange. Skin the other and cut into slices.

When the pork is cooked, remove from saucepan and slice. Place the slices on a hot serving-dish, and round them arrange the slices of orange.

Strain the sauce through a cheese cloth to clear the fat and pour into a small saucepan. Add the orange juice and a thin paste of arrowroot to thicken. Cook gently for five or six minutes, keeping well stirred and then pour over the meat. Decorate with the orange skin *julienne*.

CHAMPIGNONS MORNAY

¼ lb. mushrooms
2 oz. butter
Breakfastcup béchamel sauce (roux)
Grated cheese

Fry the mushrooms in the butter. Heat the *roux* and melt into it the grated cheese. Place the mushrooms in an open fire-proof dish, cover with the sauce, dust with grated Parmesan and heat under the grill for three or four minutes.

No. 2 Smoked eel
Scrambled eggs and kidney
Riz à l'amande

SMOKED EEL

Can be obtained from any fishmonger or from a delicatessen shop. Allow 4 to 6 oz. per person. Serve with *Sauce béarnaise*. (See page 62.)

September

SCRAMBLED EGGS AND KIDNEY

2 *lamb's kidneys*
5 *eggs*
1 *oz. butter*
2 *slices toast*
Salt, pepper

Split, wash and clean the kidneys as already advised. Soak them for ten minutes in a little water to which a teaspoon of vinegar has been added. Remove, dry and salt and pepper, Grill for not more than six minutes so that the flesh is still slightly pink. While the kidneys are grilling, beat the eggs lightly; salt and pepper to taste. Place in a small saucepan in which half the butter has been melted. Keep stirring with a wooden spoon over a very low flame. As soon as the eggs are of the right consistency, take them off the flame, add the remains of the butter in small lumps and stir again. The toast should have been placed on separate hot plates and the kidneys placed on top.

Pour the scrambled eggs over the kidneys and serve at once.

RIZ À L'AMANDE

2 *tablespoons Patna rice*
2 *tablespoons peeled and chopped almonds*
½ *pint milk*
¼ *powdered gelatine*
1 *teacup cream*
Small quantity crushed vanilla
Tablespoon sugar
Rum or port wine to flavour

Cook the rice very gently in the milk with the vanilla for three-quarters of an hour. When cooked, add the sugar, drain and leave to cool. Melt the gelatine over a low flame and stir into the rice. Then add the chopped almonds and the flavouring. Stir very gently. Place the mixture in the bowl in which it is going to be served and stir in the whipped cream very thoroughly until the mixture starts to set. Place in the lower part of the refrigerator until ready to serve.

September

No. 3 John Dory, Sauce Hollandaise
Croquettes Grand'mère
Apple Flan

JOHN DORY À L'HOLLANDAISE

John Dory is an excellent fish, much despised because of its ugly appearance. It is in consequence reasonably cheap.

1 *lb. filleted John Dory*
Fish stock
Hollandaise sauce. (See page 56.)

Place the fish in the stock, bring to the boil and cook for fifteen minutes. You will have made the sauce during this period. If delayed keep the fish warm. Serve the sauce separately.

CROQUETTES GRAND'MÈRE

½ *lb. finely chopped calf's tongue, cooked*
½ *lb. diced fried shoulder of pork*
1 *onion finely sliced*
1 *egg*
2 *oz. butter*
1 *tablespoon oil*
Breadcrumbs, flour, salt, pepper

Fry the onion in part of butter and then mix well with the tongue, pork, egg, breadcrumbs, salt and pepper. Add a little water to the mixture and knead until a good consistency is obtained. Form the croquettes and roll them in the flour to the desired shape.

Heat the butter with the oil in a frying-pan and brown the croquettes. Serve with tomato sauce.

APPLE FLAN

Short pastry
2 *cooking apples*
2 *tablespoons sugar*
Teaspoon lemon juice

Line a flan dish with the pastry. Boil the apples, but while still firm peel and core. Reheat in a saucepan with one spoonful of

133

September

sugar and just cover with water until soft and pale gold in colour.
Then place in layers in the flan dish, cover with sugar and cook
in a hot oven for twenty-five minutes.

No. 4 POTAGE FERMIÈRE

STEAK TARTARE

LOGANBERRY FLUMMERY

POTAGE FERMIÈRE

Chicken stock from the giblets and carcass of a roast bird previously eaten
1 *large potato* ⎤
1 *leek*
1 *turnip*   ⎬ *sliced*
2 *carrots*
1 *large onion* ⎦
2 *chopped tender cabbage leaves*
2 *oz. butter*
Salt, pepper

In the stock place the leek after it has been well washed, and
add the potato. Cover and simmer for an hour.

Melt the butter in a saucepan and add the rest of the vegetables.
Cover and cook over a low flame for fifteen minutes. Then add
them to the stock, cover and simmer for another fifteen minutes.
Then take out all the vegetables, and either rub them through a
sieve or make into a *purée* in an electric mixer. Return to the saucepan, bring gently to the boil, and serve.

STEAK TARTARE

½ *lb. tender rump steak finely minced*
1 *egg yolk*
1 *tablespoon chopped onion*
½ *tablespoon chopped parsley*
½ *tablespoon tomato ketchup*
6 *capers*
1 *teaspoon olive oil*
Worcestershire sauce, tabasco, salt, pepper

Place the raw meat on a plate, make a hollow and in it put the

September

oil and the raw egg-yolk. Around the meat arrange capers, parsley, and chopped onions. I warn you! In Brussels it is called Steak *américaine*. My wife and I ate some and we have never forgotten the result. But it is a popular and somewhat unusual dish, so why not try it?

LOGANBERRY FLUMMERY

½ *lb. loganberries*
1 *oz. caster sugar*
1 *tablespoon cornflour*

Stew the loganberries until soft. Then pass through a sieve, removing the pips. Place the liquid in a double saucepan and heat until the water boils. Add the sugar and the cornflour already dissolved in water. Cook for another three minutes and then pour into a mould to cool. Serve with whipped cream.

No. 5 FILLETS OF SEA BREAM
POULET FLAMBÉ
STEWED BLACKBERRIES

SEA BREAM

1 *lb. fillets*
1 *white of egg*
2 *oz. butter*
2 *tablespoons oil*
Breadcrumbs, flour, salt, pepper

Mix the breadcrumbs with flour to which pepper has been added. Dip the fillets in the beaten white of egg and then in the flour and breadcrumbs. Spread some salt on the bottom of a frying-pan and in the butter and oil fry the fish. The tip here is that the salt should prevent the fish from sticking to the pan, and the oil prevents the butter from burning. Serve with small boiled potatoes.

September

POULET FLAMBÉ

1 *small roasting chicken*
⅓ pint cream
1 *oz. butter*
Wineglass brandy

Place the chicken in melted butter in a saucepan. Heat quickly so that it browns nicely. Then cover and allow to simmer for the best part of an hour. Remove and carve.

Place the bits back in the saucepan, and increase the heat. Warm the brandy in a spoon until it catches fire. Then pour brandy on the chicken, and stir well. Take out the meat and keep hot. Add the cream slowly to the gravy in the saucepan. Do not let it boil, and stir till the sauce thickens. Season to taste. Then place the slices of chicken on a hot dish, cover with the sauce and serve.

The chicken carcass, bones and bits can be used to make good stock.

STEWED BLACKBERRIES

The 'Devil's fruit', as the old peasants used to call it, is now at its best.

1½ *lb. blackberries*
2 *tablespoons sugar*
1 *tablespoon blackberry syrup*. (There are some good brands sold in bottle.)

Cook the blackberries until they are soft, remove from the saucepan, and add to the juice the sugar and syrup. Serve the fruit in an open dish covered with the juice and syrup.

No. 6 CHICORY SALAD
CANARD AUX PÊCHES
HERRING FILLETS, CURRY SAUCE

It may seem odd to start the meal with a salad, but try this one.

136

September

CHICORY SALAD

3 fresh, firm stems of Belgian chicory
1 diced beetroot
¼ lb. blanched walnuts
Vinaigrette sauce. (See page 59.)

Dice the beetroot, cut the walnuts in half, wash and dry the chicory (the French call them endives) and cut into large slices.

Mix the ingredients together in a salad bowl, place in the refrigerator, and serve cold.

CANARD AUX PÊCHES

1 small duck
2 large fresh peaches
2 tablespoons brandy
1 oz. butter mixed with dessertspoon flour
Croûtons, salt, pepper

Salt and pepper the duck and roast for thirty minutes in a hot oven (Regulo 7) or preferably on a spit for twenty-five minutes.

Poach the peaches, halved, in sugar water.

Remove the duck, pour the fat into a pan, and mix in the butter piece by piece, and the brandy. Bring to the boil and allow to reduce by about one-third. Then pass through a sieve, taste and season as necessary.

Carve the duck and arrange the pieces on the hot croûtons which have been fried in very hot oil.

Place the halved peaches, from which the stones have been removed, around the duck meat, and pour on the sauce.

HERRING FILLETS—CURRY SAUCE

4 fresh herring fillets
1 oz. butter
Tablespoon curry powder
Dash garlic salt, salt, pepper, teacup milk

Fry the fillets in the butter. Remove from the pan, to which add the curry powder, garlic salt, salt and pepper to taste. Stir briskly until the sauce thickens. Add milk if it gets too thick. Re-heat the fillets, place them on toast fingers, and pour on the sauce.

OCTOBER MENUS

At this season Jerusalem artichokes are available. So are many kinds of game.

Try this menu.

No. 1 POTAGE PALESTINE
      ROAST PHEASANT WITH CHESTNUT STUFFING
      CRÊPES SUZETTE

POTAGE PALESTINE

½ lb. Jerusalem artichokes
2 medium-sized onions—chopped
3 oz. butter
½ pint boiled milk, ½ pint cold milk
Tablespoon flour
2 yolks of egg
¼ pint cream
Croûtons, salt and pepper, teaspoon sugar

Peeling these artichokes is a laborious job that is only necessary if it is desired to keep the soup white in colour. Personally I only give them a good soaking, scrub them well with a hard brush, and then dry them and chop them up finely.

Melt the butter in a saucepan with a thick bottom, add the onions and cook for three minutes slowly. Put in the chopped artichokes and simmer gently, stirring from time to time with a wooden spoon, for about fifteen minutes. Then add ½ pint of warm water, salt and sugar. Bring quickly to the boil. Then cover and leave to simmer for twenty minutes. Rub the mixture through a sieve. Rinse out the saucepan and put the *purée* back. Add the boiled milk and mix with the wooden spoon. Then add the cold milk in which the flour has been dissolved. Bring to the boil again and keep stirring. Then allow to simmer for five minutes. Remove from the flame, stir in the egg-yolks and cream. Strain through a sieve, re-heat if necessary, and serve with the *croûtons*.

ROAST PHEASANT

The cock pheasant is more expensive than a hen. I have yet to discover the difference in taste. A young hen is delicious.

1 *pheasant*
½ *lb. chestnuts*
1 *shallot*
3 *slices fat bacon*

Clean and truss the pheasant. Boil the chestnuts with the shallot and stuff the pheasant with the mixture. Lard the bird with the bacon and roast for forty minutes in an oven at Regulo 6 or preferably on the spit until the escape of liquid from the bird indicates that it is done.

CRÊPES SUZETTE

¼ *lb. groats*
1 *oz. caster sugar*
1 *egg*
½ *pint milk*
Salt

Mix the sugar, salt and groats and sieve into a bowl. Make a hollow and pour in an egg. With the wooden spoon stir until well mixed. Then add the milk and beat with a whisk until a smooth paste results. Leave for an hour. Just before cooking add two coffee-spoons curaçao and of orange juice.

Cook the pancakes in a shallow frying-pan, making sure it is hot before pouring in the mixture.

Brown slightly on both sides and as each pancake is cooked, place it on a hot dish. When the mixture is used up, spread each pancake with melted butter, fold into a three-cornered shape, add lemon juice, more curaçao to taste, *flambé* and serve.

No. 2 BISQUE D'HOMARD
CANETON AU RAISIN
YOGHOURT AND FRUIT JUICE

BISQUE D'HOMARD

This can be bought in sachets and produced with little trouble. To do the job properly some care must be taken.

1 *small cooked lobster*
1½ *pints fish stock*
2 *carrots*
2 *onions*
2 *shallots*
2 *sprigs parsley*
1 *sprig thyme*
1 *bay leaf*
1 *oz. butter*
2 *tablespoons flour*

Take the meat out of the lobster shell and pound in a mortar until it is really finely shredded. Meanwhile cook the vegetables and herbs in the stock until soft. Pass through a sieve. Add a wineglass of white wine, a tablespoon of brandy, and the flour. Mix well. In the sauce thus prepared place the pounded lobster and allow to cook gently for ten minutes. Remove any scum that forms. Then rub through a sieve so as to form a really smooth *purée*. Replace in the saucepan, heat and dab with small knobs of butter. Salt and pepper to taste and serve.

CANETON AU RAISIN

1 *small duck*
1 *lb. small potatoes*
1 *wineglass brandy*
2 *wineglasses burgundy*
4 *oz. butter*
2 *oz. stoned raisins*
Salt, pepper, tablespoon oil

Heat the brandy until it flames and pour it over the duck. In a casserole melt 2 oz. butter, add the duck and cook on a low flame until it is brown—about fifteen minutes. Pour the wine over the duck, salt and pepper and add the raisins which have been washed and soaked. Cover and cook in a hot oven (Regulo 7) for three-quarters of an hour. Keep an eye on the duck, and when just *saignant* put on the serving-dish. Meanwhile the potatoes, thinly sliced, have been cooking in 2 oz. of butter very slowly. Add a tablespoon of oil to prevent the butter burning, if necessary. Pass the sauce in the casserole through a sieve, check the seasoning and serve with the duck and potatoes.

YOGHOURT AND FRUIT JUICE

2 *cartons yoghourt*
1 *tablespoon fruit juice—redcurrant or raspberry*

Mix the yoghourt with the juice, chill and serve in fruit glasses.

No. 3 SPINACH SOUP
CURRIED FILLETS OF TURBOT
COLD LEMON SOUFFLÉ

SPINACH SOUP

1 *lb. fresh spinach*
1 *oz. butter*
2 *shallots*
2 *tablespoons cream*
Salt, pepper

Cook the spinach with the two shallots until soft, drain and reserve 1 pint of the stock. If you have a mixer feed the spinach leaves into it in small quantities and make a *purée*. Place the *purée* in a saucepan, add the stock, the butter, cream and seasoning and cook gently for ten minutes. Serve with *croûtons*. If no mixer then rub the spinach leaves through a sieve.

CURRIED FILLETS OF TURBOT

1 *lb. turbot fillets*
2 *large tomatoes peeled, drained and chopped*
3 *shallots*
Wineglass white wine
2 *tablespoons cream*
2 *teaspoons curry powder*
Garlic salt, salt and pepper
2 *oz. butter*

October

. Cook the shallots in butter. Salt and pepper the fillets and put into a fire-proof casserole. To the shallots add the curry powder and garlic salt, mix and pour on the fish. Add the tomatoes, pour in the wine and dab with pats of butter. Cook in a medium oven (Regulo 5) uncovered for about ten minutes. Baste well. Then add the cream and cook for a further ten minutes. Remove the fish and keep hot. Reduce the sauce until it begins to thicken. Place the fillets on the serving-dish and pour on it the curry sauce. Boiled rice can be added to this dish, but I am against this idea. It would be rather a mushy affair to eat.

COLD LEMON SOUFFLÉ

2 *lemons*
5 *eggs*
5 *oz. sugar*

Squeeze the lemons and reserve the juice. Separate the eggs, beat the yolks with the sugar and stir in the lemon juice. Place the liquid in a double saucepan so that it does not boil, and stir till it begins to thicken. Whisk the whites and fold into the mixture.
Turn into a fruit dish and freeze.

No. 4 ŒUFS SUR LE PLAT
TAGLIATELLI VERDI
STUFFED TOMATOES PROVENÇALE

OEUFS SUR LE PLAT

2 *eggs*
Teacup meat stock well seasoned and browned

Cover the bottom of two fire-proof dishes of small size with about ¼-inch of the stock. Break the eggs into the dishes and cook in a medium oven until the eggs have set. Decorate with chopped parsley.

October

TAGLIATELLI VERDI

½ *lb. tagliatelli*
2 *slices cooked ham cut in strips*
2 *large mushrooms, peeled and sliced*
2 *oz. butter*
1 *egg yolk*
Cheese sauce
Breadcrumbs, salt and pepper

Unless the tagliatelli are quite fresh they will require from twelve to fifteen minutes' boiling in salt water with a bay leaf. While they are cooking, fry the mushrooms lightly in butter and prepare the cheese sauce. For this make a thick *roux* in which the egg-yolk and grated Gruyère and Parmesan cheese (about two tablespoons of each) are incorporated.

In a buttered and hot fire-proof dish place one layer of the tagliatelli, and on it a layer of ham. Next another layer of tagliatelli and then the mushrooms. One more layer of the *pasta* followed by one of ham, and then finish with the last of the *pasta*. Pour on the sauce, sprinkle with a little Parmesan and breadcrumbs and a few dabs of butter. Place under the grill until nicely brown and serve.

STUFFED TOMATOES PROVENÇALE

2 *large tomatoes*
2 *oz. sausage meat*
1 *shallot, parsley and chervil chopped*
1 *oz. butter*
Garlic salt, breadcrumbs, salt and pepper
Tablespoon oil

Take the top off the tomatoes and empty them of the stem, seeds and liquid. Soften the shallot in butter. Mix the sausage meat with the shallot, garlic salt, herbs, salt and pepper. With this stuff the tomatoes. To cook, pour the oil into a fire-proof dish and heat. Sprinkle the tomatoes with breadcrumbs, put a dab of butter on top, place in the hot oil and cook in a medium oven (Regulo 5) for twenty minutes.

October

No. 5 VICHYSSOISE
ROAST PARTRIDGE
CRÈME CHANTILLY

VICHYSSOISE

This is in fact potato soup.

3 *leeks*
1 *onion*
4 *potatoes, peeled and sliced fine*
1 *pint chicken stock*
⅓ *pint cream*
2 *oz. butter*
Chopped watercress or chives
Salt, pepper

Chop finely the white part of the leeks and the onion. Cook for three minutes in the butter. Add the sliced potatoes and the chicken stock. Simmer in a covered saucepan for fifteen minutes, until the vegetables are soft. If you have an electric mixer put the vegetables through it. If not, rub through a fine sieve. To the *purée* add the cream, the watercress or chives, and re-heat, or if preferred, serve it chilled.

ROAST PARTRIDGE

This wonderful bird needs no special sauce or stuffing. When skilfully roasted and well basted it is a joy to the experienced diner. Spit roasted until nicely brown, basted at regular intervals with butter and its own juices, and salted and peppered, it is to my mind the king of game birds. Do not hang it too long after you have bought it or have been given it by a sporting friend. Partridge does not gain by the early stages of putrefaction, as some game does. Nevertheless, in cool weather it can wait for a week before cooking.

If a spit is not available, roast in the usual way in a medium oven (Regulo 5) twenty minutes for each pound weight. Baste frequently. Serve with chip potatoes, breadcrumbs and its own gravy.

A green salad with a French dressing is an admirable adjunct.

October

CRÈME CHANTILLY

Meringue cases can be bought from most bakers. Fill with whipped cream to which a dash of some liqueur has been added and sugar to taste.

No. 6 POTAGE GARBURE
CRABE À LA MODE DE TAMBLYN
PECAN DELIGHTS

POTAGE GARBURE

1 *pint stock*
1 *carrot*
1 *turnip*
3 *leeks—the white only*
A quarter of a small cabbage
2 *sticks celery*
4 *oz. butter*
2 *medium potatoes*
Teaspoon chervil
Croûtons
Grated cheese

Chop the vegetables fairly small. Heat 2 oz. butter in a saucepan and cook the vegetables in it slowly. Add salt and a pinch of sugar. After thirty minutes add ¾ pint of the stock and bring to the boil. Cover and cook slowly for three-quarters of an hour. When the vegetables are soft pass them through a sieve or make into a *purée* in an electric mixer. Thin this *purée* to the necessary consistency with the balance of the stock. Bring back to the boil. Remove and add the chervil and then pour into a heat-proof bowl. Cover the surface of the soup with rounds of French bread and on these scatter the grated cheese. Add small dabs of butter to each round and place under the grill until the cheese begins to brown. Serve.

CRAB TAMBLYN (CRABE À LA MODE DE TAMBLYN)

This is a concoction devised by a private individual. For those who like crab it sounds excellent!

K   145

October

½ *lb. cooked flaked crab-meat, either fresh or tinned*
3 eggs
Breakfastcup rice
Grated cheese
Cream

Place the crab-meat in a buttered fire-proof dish and moisten with two tablespoons cream. Beat the eggs ready for scrambling. Boil the rice, strain, wash and dry.

Scramble the eggs lightly and add to the crab-meat; cover with grated cheese and place under the grill for two minutes.

Serve the rice separately.

PECAN DELIGHTS (By the same inventor.)

2 oz. butter
Tablespoon sugar
½ *breakfastcup ground almonds, unblanched*
Teaspoon vanilla
¼ *breakfastcup flour*
Pecan nuts (which can now be bought in most big stores).

Cream the butter, add sugar, almonds, vanilla and flour and mix thoroughly. Shape the mixture into disks ½-inch thick and 2 inches in diameter. Place half a pecan nut on each and arrange on a buttered baking-dish. Cook in a moderate oven (Regulo 5) for thirty minutes. Cool, and dust thickly with icing sugar.

NOVEMBER MENUS

No. 1 CHICKEN LIVERS
SCALLOP KEBAB
BABA AU RHUM

CHICKEN LIVERS

6 *chicken livers*
1 *onion chopped*
2 *oz. butter*
Salt, pepper

Cook the livers lightly in the butter, salt and pepper to taste. Add the onion, cook for another ten minutes and serve very hot, with toast fingers.

SCALLOP KEBAB

¾ *lb. scallops*
6 *small rashers streaky bacon*
1 *large onion*
2 *oz. butter*
Chopped parsley
Toast

Place the scallops for two minutes in boiling salt water. Drain and dry them thoroughly. Melt the butter in a pan and in it dip the scallops. Remove and set aside. Parboil the onion previously and cut into rings thick enough to hold together. Skewer the scallops, the bacon, and the onion rings alternately. Grill until the bacon is cooked (about six minutes), remove from the skewers and place on the toast. Sprinkle with the chopped parsley and serve with Sauce Robert. (See page 62.)

BABA AU RHUM

The simplest way to achieve this sweet is to buy the *baba* (a ring of spongy *brioche*) from your pastrycook.

Prepare a syrup by boiling three ounces of caster sugar in a teacup of water. Cool and add a claret-glass of rum. Set aside. An hour before serving sprinkle the *baba* with the syrup drop by drop until it is soaked but still firm. Serve with whipped cream in the centre of the ring.

No. 2   Shrimp cocktail
Chicken paella
Apple slices with honey

SHRIMP COCKTAIL

1 *small package peeled shrimps*
2 *lettuce leaves*
⅛ *pint mayonnaise*

Wash the shrimps. Chop the lettuce leaves and cover the bottom of a fruit-glass. When the shrimps are dry, place them on the lettuce and cover with the *mayonnaise*. (See page 56.)

CHICKEN PAELLA

A Spanish dish—rather filling!
Wings of chicken can now be bought in most butchers' shops.

4 *wings*
¾ *pint chicken stock*
2 *small onions*
2 *red or green peppers*
½ *teacup rice*
¼ *lb. mushrooms*
4 *tomatoes, peeled, seeded, and emptied*
Dash garlic salt, pinch of saffron, pepper and salt

Any green vegetables such as peas and beans left over from a previous meal can be added.

Slice onions and peppers finely and brown in hot oil. Add the meat from the chicken wings, the mushrooms (sliced) and the rice. Pour on the chicken stock. Slice the tomatoes and add with any green vegetables available, and the saffron. Now simmer very slowly until the liquid is absorbed into the rice which should still not be too soft. Time, fifteen minutes or more.

November

APPLE SLICES WITH HONEY

The Roman gourmet Apicius would have liked this sweet, with its contrasting tastes and its use of honey.

2 large cooking apples—Bramleys or Jonathans
1 oz. butter
1 soup-spoon honey
½ teacup whipped cream
Dash cinnamon

Core and slice the apples ½-inch thick. Cover one side of each slice with a layer of butter and lay in a buttered pan, butter side down. Spread the honey on the top side and place under the grill for seven minutes.

Whip the cream with the cinnamon and serve separately.

NO. 3 PURÉE DE MARRONS
BRAISED PHEASANT
ORANGE JELLY

PURÉE DE MARRONS

½ lb. chestnuts
1 oz. butter
1 pint stock
Small stick celery
1 lump sugar

Peel the chestnuts and place them in a small saucepan with the celery cut small, half the stock and the lump of sugar. Bring to the boil, cover and leave to simmer until the chestnuts are soft right through. This will take at least three-quarters of an hour, perhaps longer. When ready, rub the chestnuts and sauce through a sieve, or preferably beat in an electric mixer. Place the *purée* back in the saucepan and stir briskly with a whisk. As you beat add the balance of the stock until the right consistency is achieved. Then bring again to the boil, still stirring. Leave to simmer, clearing off the scum from time to time. When ready remove from the flame, add the butter bit by bit, and serve with *croûtons*.

November

BRAISED PHEASANT

Somebody may send you an oldish cock pheasant. It will best be cooked in the following manner:

1 *pheasant*
1 *thin slice salt pork or fat bacon*
1 *tangerine orange*
¼ *lb. mushrooms*
2 *oz. butter*
1 *small onion or 2 shallots*
2 *teaspoons flour*
Claret-glass Marsala or Madeira
Salt, pepper, origanum or dried parsley.

Lift the skin on the bird's breast and insert the slice of pork or bacon. Stuff the bird with its own liver and the peeled tangerine. Sow up or pin the body cavity. Heat a pan of oil and roll the pheasant in this until it is golden colour. Remove to a heated casserole.

In the melted butter cook the mushrooms lightly and add them to the casserole. In the same pan put the chopped onion or shallots with the flour and cook but do not allow to brown. To this add the wine slowly, stirring all the time. If the amount of liquid appears insufficient add a little of the oil in which the bird was browned. Add salt and pepper and the herbs. Add this mixture to the casserole, cover and cook in an oven (Regulo 6) for at least an hour.

ORANGE JELLY

4 *oranges*
Dessertspoon sugar
Dessertspoon gelatine
Dessertspoon orange curaçao or cointreau

Cut the peel of two oranges in the form of two 'baskets' with a handle. Carefully remove the pulp so that the 'baskets' are undamaged. Peel the other oranges and remove the inner skin. Squeeze the juice out of the pulp and mix with the liqueur. Dissolve the gelatine and mix with the orange very thoroughly. Fill the baskets with the mixture and set aside to cool and set.

No. 4 Game Soup
Lamb Chops (Provençale)
Gnocchi

GAME SOUP

You will certainly have saved the sauce and bits from the braised pheasant. With the addition of stock these remains, with two or three braised shallots, can be put through a mixer or a sieve to make an excellent game soup.

LAMB CUTLETS PROVENÇALE

4 *lamb cutlets*
5 *tomatoes*
2 *oz. butter*
Garlic salt, chervil and parsley chopped
Salt and pepper

Cut the tomatoes in half, across the stem, clean them and insert small pieces of butter. Sprinkle herbs, garlic salt, salt and pepper over them.

On the grill, place the cutlets and the tomatoes, the cutlets nearest to you so that you can turn them more easily. The tomatoes may take longer than the meat to grill, so watch this point.

GNOCCHI

2 *large potatoes*
¼ *lb. mushrooms, sliced*
1 *egg.*
1 *oz. butter*
Teaspoon lemon juice
2 *tablespoons flour*
Salt, pepper

Peel and cook the potatoes as if to make a *purée*. Wash the mushrooms thoroughly in water with a teaspoon vinegar. Dry and slice small. Slice and dry the cooked potatoes. Mash them and mix with the egg, flour and butter, proceeding with small quantities to get thorough incorporation with the potato. Add salt and pepper and heat very thoroughly.

Roll this dough out into a thin sausage, cut off small pieces and flatten slightly. Prick with a fork. Sprinkle with a little flour and plunge into boiling salt water. In a few minutes the *gnocchi* should swell and rise to the surface, when they can be removed, strained and placed on a hot dish.

Meanwhile the chopped mushrooms have been frying in butter for a few minutes. Add to them the lemon juice and spread them over the *gnocchi* with the melted butter.

No. 5 POTAGE CRECY
TOURNEDOS GRILLÉS, SAUCE BÉARNAISE
COMPOTE D'ABRICOTS À LA CRÈME

POTAGE CRECY

½ *lb. carrots*
1 *medium-size onion chopped fine*
3 *oz. butter*
1 *pint good stock cleared of fat*
Sprig parsley, dessertspoon sugar, chervil

Clean the carrots and slice along their length, taking care to avoid any hard yellow centres. Braise with the chopped onion in two ounces of butter. Take the crust off the top of a small white loaf, leaving about half an inch of the bread under the crust. Chop into lumps about an inch cube, and dry in the oven, but do not brown. Mix the sugar with the braised vegetables and then add two-thirds of the stock and the parsley. Bring to the boil, cover and simmer for forty minutes. Meanwhile prepare the *croûtons*.

Rub the soup through a sieve, and replace in the saucepan. Add the rest of the stock. Bring again to the boil and then allow to simmer for fifteen minutes, removing any scum that forms. Then add the rest of the butter piece by piece and the chervil with the saucepan away from the flame. Pass once more through the sieve, reheat and serve with the *croûtons*.

November

TOURNEDOS GRILLÉS—SAUCE BÉARNAISE

2 *nice fillets steak, about 6 oz. each*
Parsley butter
Sauce béarnaise. (See page 62)

Grill the fillets three minutes on each side. Decorate with the parsley butter.

Serve separately from the sauce.

COMPÔTE D'ABRICOTS

¾ *lb. dried apricots*
⅓ *pint cream*
Tablespoon kirsch or brandy

Soak the apricots until well softened—about five or six hours.

Place them in a saucepan and just cover with hot water. Add two soup-spoons of sugar and cook for twenty minutes. Allow to cool. Cover with the cream to which the liqueur has been added and serve.

Try a vegetarian meal of a rather unusual type.

No. 6 INTUBA ET LACTUCAE

CHOU ROUGE AUX MARRONS

WALNUT PURÉE

ENDIVE AND LETTUCE À LA ROMAINE

Endives and lettuce should still be available.

2 *endives* (*Belgian chicory*)
1 *lettuce* (*cos or cabbage*)

'Dress the lettuce and chicory with vinegar and a little fish stock (liquamen) to make them more digestible, to prevent flatulence and so the lettuces cannot harm your system. Add 1 oz. cummin, ½ oz. ginger, ½ fresh rue, ¼ oz. juicy dates, ½ oz. pepper, 4½ oz. honey, well pounded and mixed.'

Aren't you glad you did not live in Roman times?

I suggest as an alternative chopping the vegetables coarsely and serving with a light *mayonnaise* dressing.

November

CHOU ROUGE AUX MARRONS

Red cabbage should be available. Chestnuts are beginning to dry out.

1 *medium-sized red cabbage*
1 *lb. chestnuts*
2 *oz. bacon diced*
2 *eating apples, Granny Smith or similar*
1 *oz. butter*

Peel and skin the chestnuts. You will know the boiling water method. Cook in water for one hour or until they are tender.

Quarter the cabbage, cutting out the hard stem and coarse outer leaves. Boil till it softens. Fry the diced bacon in butter and add the chestnuts. When brown, cover with the cabbage and place the quartered apples on top. Add some of the cabbage stock (enough to prevent burning), cover and simmer for ten minutes.

WALNUT PURÉE

Fresh walnuts are delicious. Those that are dried are not, in my opinion, worth eating as nuts. But something can be done with them.

½ *lb. dried walnuts, skinned*
1 *oz. caster sugar*
1 *oz. butter*
⅓ *pint cream*
Teaspoon grated nutmeg

Blanch the walnuts and pound into a *purée*. Mix with the butter and grated nutmeg and pass through a sieve. Cook lightly for ten minutes. Allow to cool. Whip the cream and fold into the walnut mixture. Serve cold with a crystallized cherry on top.

DECEMBER MENUS

No. 1 Fonds d'artichauts Apicius
Irish stew Provençale
Prune whip

ARTICHAUTS APICIUS

This is a much more reasonable Roman recipe.

4 artichoke hearts
2 hard-boiled eggs
Teaspoon lemon juice
Vinegar, oil, pepper and salt
Parsley

If the artichokes are not already cooked, *sauté* them in oil with a dash of lemon juice. Remove and stuff with the chopped hard-boiled eggs. Decorate with chopped parsley and serve with a French dressing.

IRISH STEW PROVENÇALE

¾ lb. boned shoulder mutton
¾ lb. potatoes
6 small onions, whole
1 medium onion ⎫
¼ lb. mushrooms ⎬ *chopped*
1 carrot ⎪
1 turnip ⎭
3 or 4 leaves cabbage or one leek
1 clove garlic, bouquet garni
3 oz. butter
Dash Worcestershire sauce, salt, pepper

Cut the meat up into cubes about three-quarters of an inch in size, wash in cold water, remove and dry.

Cook the vegetables, including the garlic, in two ounces of butter, together with the *bouquet garni* in a covered saucepan until they are soft.

Meanwhile the meat has been boiled in a saucepan, in just enough water to cover it, for five minutes. Strain and cool. Replace the cleaned saucepan, add the vegetables, with salt and pepper and cover again with water and simmer gently for three-quarters of an hour. Then add the potatoes which have been sliced and give the whole another half-hour of gentle cooking. Fish out the meat with a perforated spoon and set aside in a heated serving-dish. Pass the vegetables through a sieve or a mixer to make a *purée*. While this is going on, cook the small onions and mushrooms in the rest of the butter. Remember that the mushrooms cook more quickly than the onions. Add them to the *purée* of vegetables and season with salt, pepper and Worcestershire sauce to taste.

Pour on to the meat and re-heat. Whole boiled potatoes sprinkled with chopped parsley can be used as garnish.

PRUNE WHIP

½ *lb. prunes*
2 *whites of egg*
Dash of lemon juice
1 *oz. sugar*
1 *teaspoon grated lemon rind*
⅓ *pint cream*

Soak and stone the prunes and put them through the electric mixer with a little water to make a stiff pulp. Whip the egg-whites firmly. Add the lemon juice to the prune pulp, and then fold in the whipped egg. Add the grated lemon rind. Place the whole in a small baking-dish and set in a dish of hot water. Cook in a slow oven (Regulo 4) until the mixture is firm. Serve cold with whipped cream.

No. 2 PAUPIETTES DE SOLE
COQ AU VIN
MACAROON SOUFFLÉ

December

PAUPIETTE DE SOLE—SAUCE HOLLANDAISE

4 sole fillets
1 oz. butter
1 wineglass white wine

Poach the fillets for ten minutes. Roll the fillets and tie them with string. Simmer for ten minutes in the butter and white wine. Remove the string, place the fish on the serving-dish, pour over them the white wine and butter and serve separately with the *hollandaise*. (See page 56.)

COQ AU VIN

1 small chicken
2 oz. butter
4 oz, lard
1 onion, chopped
4 small mushrooms, chopped
2 wineglasses red wine
Salt, pepper, mixed herbs

Cut the chicken into wings, legs and breast. Melt the butter and lard in a saucepan, and cook the chicken in the mixture until it is nicely golden brown; about thirty minutes as a rule. Add the onion and herbs and mushrooms, and the red wine. Allow to simmer for another thirty minutes—do not cover. When the liquid is almost completely reduced add the butter mixed with a dash of flour. As soon as the butter is melted, serve the chicken, pouring over it the gravy.

MACAROON SOUFFLÉ

6 macaroons (bought at your baker's)
2 egg-yolks
Teacup boiled milk
1 tablespoon rum
2 egg-whites
Dash salt
1 tin litchis in syrup

Pour the hot milk over the macaroons. When they are soft beat into a *purée* and add the egg-yolk. Thicken the mixture in the bain-marie or double saucepan. Leave to cool. Then add the rum. Beat

December

the egg-whites with the salt until they are stiff. Fold into the macaroon mixture. Turn into a small baking-dish, set in a pan of water and cook for thirty minutes in the oven at Regulo 6. Turn out on to the serving dish, garnish with the litchis and serve.

No. 3 POTAGE PRINCE DE GALLES
PERDRIX AUX CHOUX
WINE CUSTARD

POTAGE PRINCE DE GALLES

Giolitto of Quaglinos prepared this delicious soup for me on many occasions. I have not been able to trace it in any cookery book that I have consulted. Here is my recollection of how he would make it.

1 *pint strong veal stock, flavoured with herbs*
2 *egg-yolks*
1 *wineglass sherry*

Beat the egg-yolks into the hot, but not boiling, stock. Bring to the point of boiling. Add the sherry. Serve. The liquid must not boil. A further precaution to prevent a scrambled egg 'mess' would be to add a coffee-spoon of arrowroot. There is, I am told, a thick soup called *Potage Prince de Galles*, but it is not the same thing.

PERDRIX AUX CHOUX

1 *young partridge*
1 *lb. cabbage*
4 *oz. lard*
1 *sausage (raw)*
3 *slices fat bacon*
¼ *lb. carrots*
1 *large onion stuck with a clove*
Bouquet garni
1 *pint stock*
Arrowroot
2 *oz. butter*

158

December

This recipe means two and a half hours of work—on and off! The partridge will have been prepared, so start on the cabbage. Wash and dry the leaves, pepper and salt them lightly. In a tall saucepan heat the lard and braise the bird lightly—five minutes on its back and four minutes for each side. Remove and set aside. Cover the bottom of the saucepan with the bacon. On the bacon place a thick layer of cabbage—about one-third of the whole. On the cabbage place the partridge, with the carrots, cleaned and peeled but not cut up, around it. Another layer of cabbage follows, on top of which go some more lard, the sausage, the onion and the *bouquet garni*. One last layer of cabbage and then the stock which should cover the bird, but not necessarily the vegetables. Bring to the boil and cover. Simmer for thirty minutes and then remove the sausage, the bacon, and the bird. Set aside and keep warm. Transfer the cabbage and stock to a fire-proof dish and finish in the oven (Regulo 6) for another hour. At the end of this time, cut the bacon into small squares, slice the sausage and the carrots finely. Then put the cabbage into a sieve, pressing it with a spoon so that the liquid goes back into the dish, remove the onion and the *bouquet garni*, and place the cabbage in a mound on the serving-dish. On top goes the partridge and round it the carrots, the sausage and the bacon. Keep hot.

Into a small saucepan pour the liquid from the fire-proof dish. Reduce by boiling briskly. Watch that it does not become too salt. Thicken with a little flour, add browning to colour, and complete with the butter away from the flame. Pour some of the gravy over the bird and serve the rest separately.

WINE CUSTARD

1 *claret-glass white wine*
2 *eggs*
Tablespoon sugar

In a bain-marie place the wine and half the quantity of water. Add the eggs and sugar—beat briskly while heating until the mixture begins to thicken. Keep on beating until cooking is complete—about ten minutes. Serve either hot or cold.

December

Christmas is with us. A rich and savoury dinner seems indicated —but not turkey or goose. Too ordinary.

No. 4 HELFORD RIVER OYSTERS

BŒUF STROGANOFF

CHRISTMAS LOG

HELFORD RIVER OYSTERS

To my mind a dozen Helford river oysters, with brown bread and butter, lemon or vinegar and a dash of cayenne are an excellent start to a good meal.

BEEF STROGANOFF

A simple and pleasant way of doing rump steak.

¾ lb. rump steak
3 shallots
3 oz. butter
¼ pint cream

Cut the steak into fine slices and braise for five minutes in butter. Salt and pepper and add the finely chopped shallots. When the shallots are soft add the cream, mix well and serve.

CHRISTMAS LOG

1 lb. chestnuts
2 oz. cooking chocolate
2 oz. sugar
2 oz. butter

Boil the chestnuts for a few minutes, plunge in cold water and peel, including the inner skin. Then boil them again for twenty minutes. Dry and crush into a *purée*. Re-heat and add the chocolate, hot and melted, the sugar and the melted butter. Stir thoroughly.

Roll the mixture in the shape of a log and place it in well-buttered greaseproof paper. Chill in the refrigerator. Remove the paper and decorate the log with any fancy design that occurs to you, and with half walnuts peeled and blanched.

160

December

No. 5 Tomatoes stuffed with spinach
Spaghetti and minced liver
Pommes alsaciennes

STUFFED TOMATOES

3 *tomatoes*
¼ *lb. spinach*
¼ *lb. cooked ham*
Grated Parmesan

The spinach can either be in a *purée* or finely chopped. Heat with butter and cream, and mix with a small quantity of minced ham. Cut the tomatoes in two, remove seeds, hard core and liquid. Stuff with the spinach and ham mixture, sprinkle with grated Parmesan and cook slowly in a moderate oven (Regulo 3) for half an hour.

SPAGHETTI AND LIVER

½ *packet long spaghetti*
½ *lb. best liver*
¼ *lb. mushrooms*
⅓ *pint cream*
1 *oz. butter*
2 *eggs*
2 *tablespoons grated Gruyère cheese*

Boil the spaghetti in salt water with two bay leaves for fifteen minutes.

Meanwhile fry the liver lightly in butter and chop fine; do the same with mushrooms, and mix the whole with the cream away from the flame. Then add the egg-yolks and the cheese, and turn the whole into a saucepan with the washed and dried spaghetti. Re-heat and serve.

L

161

December

POMMES ALSACIENNES

4 *good cooking apples*
1 *egg*
Soup-spoon flour
2 *tablespoons sugar*
Liqueur-glass kirsch
Breakfastcup milk

Peel and slice the apples and lay them in a buttered fire-proof dish. Pour on to them a sauce made by mixing the flour, egg, sugar, milk and kirsch. Cook in a medium oven (Regulo 4) for thirty-five minutes.

No. 6 CHRISTMAS DINNER

So much depends on the size of the company at table and its composition that no recommendation of mine can help. Convention too is observed by some and not by others.

If the meal was to be served in my home to my wife and family it would be more or less as below:

Caviar rolled in smoked salmon, with sliced lemon. Vodka.
Roast partridge, chipolata sausages, *sauté* potatoes.
Green salad.
Cheval Blanc, 1934.
Christmas pudding, brandy butter.
Liqueurs and coffee.

CHAPTER XII

Potato Recipes

I am assuming that *pommes de terre en robe de champs* or potatoes cooked in their skins present no problem to the housewife. But another simple recipe—*purée de pommes de terre*—can be a failure, lumpy and stodgy, if certain precautions are not taken.

First of all, use the right kind of potato. Personally I prefer King Edwards. Then the method of making the *purée* has a certain importance.

First peel the potatoes and cut into quarters. Place in a saucepan with just enough salt water to cover them. Bring to the boil as quickly as possible and cook only until the potatoes are just soft enough to rub through a sieve. Dry them out thoroughly and then, in small quantities, pass through the sieve. Use plenty of elbow grease for this operation. French cooks say you should feel muscular pain in your arm for an hour after the sieving. Place the *purée* back in the saucepan and as quickly as possible so as not to let it cool, keep it stirring on a low flame while you add salt, white pepper, a pinch of nutmeg and then the butter in small lumps so that it melts evenly. Do not stir but rather beat and lift so that air gets into the mixture and makes it light. Finally add a small quantity of boiling milk before serving.

A *purée* can be served *gratinée* by placing it in a buttered dish,

Potato Recipes

covering it with breadcrumbs mixed with grated Gruyère cheese and a dressing of melted butter, and then putting it under the grill for two or three minutes.

POMMES DE TERRE DUCHESSE

This is a mixture of potato *purée* and egg. Again take a floury potato for the task. You will need two yolks of egg for each pound of peeled potatoes and two ounces of butter. Make the *purée* as already indicated and place in a thick-bottomed saucepan. Add salt, pepper and nutmeg, stirring briskly and continuously on a low flame until the *purée* begins to dry out, and becomes a thick paste. Leave to cool for two minutes and then, very gradually, add the egg-yolks, stirring all the time. Heat for two minutes, still stirring, and then pour the paste on to a buttered dish. Spread it out thinly so that it cools quickly. Wipe over with a small piece of butter to prevent it forming a crust. When it is cool use the paste to form whatever you wish, edging, croquettes or pyramids round a dish of fish or meat. They will, of course, need re-heating.

POMMES DE TERRE À LA MAÎTRE D'HÔTEL

Potatoes, milk, two ounces of butter, chopped parsley, grated nutmeg. For this recipe it is necessary to select potatoes that are farinaceous, but firm. Otherwise in the process they disintegrate and make a porridge. Place the peeled potatoes in cold salt water and bring to the boil for twenty minutes. When they are cooked, but not soft, take them out and slice them. Bring your milk to the boil in a thick-bottomed saucepan and then allow the potatoes to simmer for fifteen minutes with the parsley, nutmeg and half the butter. When ready to serve, add the rest of the butter, shaking the saucepan to mix it but not to break the slices of potato.

POMMES DE TERRE SAUTÉES

Again take potatoes that are not too floury, and boil them in their skins, making sure they are not overcooked, peel and slice.

164

Potato Recipes

Heat your butter, clarify it and then put in the sliced potatoes. Use a brisk heat until the slices are a golden brown.

POMMES DE TERRE LYONNAISE

These are *sauté* potatoes with the addition of finely sliced onion. Heat the two vegetables separately in butter until they are almost cooked and then heat them together for another three minutes. Excellent with grills.

POMMES DE TERRE AUX HARENGS

This is a useful supper dish. Cook your potatoes in their skins. Boil the herrings for ten minutes and then skin and remove the bones completely. Peel and slice your cooked potatoes and place a layer on the bottom of a well-buttered fire-proof dish. Cover with a layer of the herring meat dressed with chopped parsley, shallots, cream and a pinch of pepper. Add layers of potatoes and the herring mixture until the dish is full, finishing with a layer of potatoes, pepper, salt and pats of butter. Cook for half an hour in a moderate oven (Regulo 3) so that the dish can simmer gently and absorb all the cream.

POMMES DE TERRE FARCIES

Stuffed potatoes are also an excellent supper dish. Roast them in their skins, empty out the contents and mix with whatever odds and ends of cooked meat, ham, tongue, you may have left over. The addition of a little sausage meat is a precaution against over-dryness. Stuff the skins and heat through again.

One recipe recommends sausage meat alone, with the addition of an egg and breadcrumbs to every pound of meat. In this case the cooking time is longer. A dash of garlic salt, half a wineglass of white wine, and some chopped parsley or other herbs will improve the stuffing.

POMMES DE TERRE FARCIES À L'ARDENNAISE

This is a potato baked in its skin and stuffed with chopped ham, cheese and yolk of eggs.

Potato Recipes

Roast your potatoes, cut them in half and empty out the pulp into a well-warmed bowl. It is necessary to mix the pulp while it is really hot. Add butter and work it into the pulp. Then put in salt, pepper, nutmeg, egg-yolks in succession, stirring briskly. Then add grated cheese, ham, and chopped parsley. Place the mixture in the potato skins, powder with some more grated cheese, pour on a small quantity of melted butter and heat for twenty minutes in a moderate oven (Regulo 3).

POMMES DE TERRE SUZETTE

This is a recipe often used in good-class restaurants at home and abroad.

You will need:

3 or 4 large floury potatoes
4 oz. butter
4 oz. chicken scraps, either roast or boiled
4 oz. salt tongue or lean ham
2 or 3 small mushrooms already cooked
2 yolks of egg
A cupful of cream or 'top of the milk'
Salt, pepper and nutmeg

Peel your potatoes with a circular motion—not up and down their length. This method gives a smooth appearance as the cut does not show, and the potato looks rather like a large egg.

Cut off a slice from one end so that the potatoes can stand upright. Dry them on a cloth—don't wash them.

On a lightly buttered fire-proof dish stand the potatoes on their flattened ends. Cook them in a brisk oven (Regulo 6) until, after about thirty minutes, they are a nice golden colour. While this is going on cut up the chicken, tongue and mushrooms into small cubes.

When the potatoes are cooked slice off a small 'lid' from the top of each of them, and with a small spoon or preferably a potato-peeler, remove their centres, taking care not to damage the outer 'hull'. Do the same to the 'lids'. The pulp you have taken out is then reduced by a quarter and worked up with a wooden spoon until it is a smooth *purée*. Then add salt, pepper, nutmeg and the four ounces of butter. Mix well and then add the cream or milk, subsequently the yolk of eggs, the chicken, tongue—the lot.

With this mixture stuff the potato 'hulls' and top off with the 'lids'.

Put back in the oven to ensure uniform heating for about ten minutes. Place on a dish lined with a napkin—to prevent them sliding about—and smear them lightly with melted butter to make them look attractive!

CHIP POTATOES

These are too easy. All you must be sure of is that your oil is really hot and that the potato slices, after two good soakings in cold water, are dry. Serve quickly.

POMMES DE TERRE SOUFFLÉES

A delightful way of doing potatoes, light and digestible. But there is one point in the recipe which is of cardinal importance. The slices of raw potato that are to be *soufflé* must be clean cut and of absolutely uniform thickness. There is a tool which can almost certainly be bought in London stores (I got mine from Switzerland) which ensures this condition. It is a flat, slotted plate with an adjustable cutter in the slot. Any thickness up to ¼-inch can be cut from potatoes, cucumbers or other firm vegetables.

To succeed with this rather tricky recipe take good firm potatoes such as King Edward, of at least 1¼-inch diameter. Peel and wash them and dry them thoroughly. Slice them on the slicer at a setting that will give you pieces which are ⅛-inch thick. In your pan heat oil (maize or olive) to a moderate heat—it must not smoke and a breadcrumb thrown into it should only brown very slowly. It is essential to have a 'deep fry' so that the potatoes will not clog on each other and so defeat your purpose.

I suggest two pints of oil for enough potatoes for two people. You can always use the oil again. When the oil is sufficiently hot drop the potato slices one by one into the 'deep fry'. Gradually increase the heat until the potatoes, after about seven or eight minutes, begin to float on top of the oil. At once raise the heat sharply, when the potatoes should start to swell and turn golden.

Remove them quickly with a strainer and put them into a sieve where the surplus oil can drain off.

Then heat the oil in the 'deep fry' until it smokes. Plunge the potatoes, still in the sieve, into the boiling oil, and tip them out to float by themselves. After a minute they should be done and can be fished out with a strainer, allowed to dry, and then powdered with salt and served in a dish lined with a napkin.

CHAPTER XIII

On Vegetables

It will be noticed in the menus that very rarely are the accompanying vegetables mentioned. Only where, in my opinion, certain vegetables prepared in a particular manner are essential to the dish are they described.

Here again it is so much a matter of taste, but there are certain basic principles in the preparation of vegetables which cannot be disregarded. The first is the use of salt in the cooking water. The second is that all green vegetables should be steamed rather than boiled, i.e. cooked with a minimum of water and always covered.

It must also be remembered that vegetables can, with a certain amount of preparation, be used as a main dish, either at a summer time lunch, or for supper.

Probably the best known of these is the mixed vegetable dish of small beetroots, cauliflower, new potatoes, small onions, green peas or beans, and perhaps one or two leeks, served hot with a good cheese sauce. Then Jerusalem artichokes can be prepared in a number of ways as an accompanying vegetable. I like them boiled, sliced and also served with a cheese sauce. Aubergines (egg plant) sliced and fried with butter are excellent with meat. Both aubergines and courgettes may be steamed lightly and even dipped in thin batter, before frying. I have already mentioned

169

courgettes, but cucumber can also be used in the same way, with onions and a white sauce. Belgian endives, braised or *meunière*, can be a course or an accompanying vegetable. But every housewife or husband-cook should possess Ambrose Heath's *Good Vegetables*. There are recipes covering a hundred ways of using fresh vegetables. Forget the margarine recommended (the book came out in days of austerity) and use butter instead. The price difference is negligible and the taste much improved. I have, as Heath recommends, eaten nettles and dandelion leaves. The French do not hesitate to do so, but in Britain there are better alternatives.

Some excellent books have been published on the eating of wild fungi. On their recommendation I have experimented even to the extent of eating Inky Caps, and have lived! But of all the odd growths that have come to my table, only two have remained in my memory as a worth-while experience. These two fungi are named in France 'morelles' and 'cèpes'. In England 'morelles' have almost the same name and are sometimes called 'little owls' from their appearance. Cèpes do grow in our country, but are generally regarded as poisonous rubbish. The French know better.

My recommendation about vegetables is, then, that you should consult Ambrose Heath's book, and be as adventurous as you please in the preparation and serving of the hundreds of excellent growths that are freely available, firstly when they are fresh, and secondly as a doubtful resort—due to laziness—in frozen form. I must admit, however, that what comes out of the deep freeze is usually of very good quality. But it does just lack that delicate flavour of the product straight out of the ground.

Index

Index

Index

Index